Apparently So
By David L. Price

Illustrations by Alex Carr, Mira Dabrowski and William Bernard Keating

Cover design, layout assistance by Sarah Mattern, matternco.com

To Michelle:
Peace, love and don't you
care vote for Carly! Thanks
so much for being such a great
colleague and friend!
Big hug,
David

1

Here's a suggestion for my epitaph when the time finally comes:

"He was easy to wound, tough to kill."

In the meantime:

My enduring love and gratitude to Fátima, my children – Ellery and Owen – and my family and friends over these many years, especially these past six months, for your support and your unbridled affection. It's meant the world to me.

Apparently So
By David L. Price

Illustrations by Alex Carr, Mira Dabrowski
and William Bernard Keating

Also by David L. Price:

Slugger, *a novel*

Can she do it? Will she?

Jackie Wilson's marriage to her high-school sweetheart has dissolved into an increasingly abusive battleground as her husband acts out his life's frustrations. Told against a backdrop of professional baseball; drug addiction; the gorgeous rolling plains near Parker and Castle Rock, Colorado; and an 18-hand chestnut stallion named Leonardo.

Slugger is available in ebook or paperback versions through www.davidpriceapparentlyso.com

Apparently So
By David L. Price

Illustrations by Alex Carr, Mira Dabrowski and William Bernard Keating

Cover design, layout assistance by Sarah Mattern, matternco.com

Table of Contents

Prologue

For some strange reason I couldn't find the Los Gatos outpost where my pulmonologist examines lungs and renders verdicts. But her nurse had called and insisted the doctor wanted to see me right away. The only opening was at her Los Gatos office and that particular bastion of healthcare sits almost 20 miles from my modest chunk of the Silicon Valley housing market.

Most of the time she sees patients in her Mountain View office, which I can throw Bing cherries at and splat them off the walls from my tiny front yard.

So I drove down I-85 South towards the Highway 17 exit and took Winchester Road to the right and toward the mountains, instead of heading left toward yet another suburban mall on the other side. This made sense to me because I thought Los Gatos snuggled into the foothills leading to Santa Cruz.

Although those of us around here pronounce Los Gatos with the hard American "a," the phrase still means "the cats," of course. The name dates back to the early 1800s when the area was called "Cat's Corner," according to Wikipedia. And the cats in question were not the ones that curl up next to our bodies for warmth at night and sit on our faces and yowl when they think it's past their precious breakfast time.

Oh, no. Before we bull-dozed the land for housing, gas stations and fancy coffee shops, the cats patrolling the verdant territory were either of the "bob" variety or mountain lions. Imagine what THEY could do to your face if you happened to be late with their breakfast.

Sometimes I get annoyed at the way we pronounce Los Gatos, since I much prefer the sound of the soft "a." Then I remember my motto, the one my lovely Brazilian wife helped me come up with and that has served me quite well over the past several years: "Go Gently Through Life."

The motto means that life is so much more fulfilling when I try to live in the moment, free of fear and regret, and when I'm mindful of myself and my actions at all times. The point is to try to glide through life like a pod of bottlenose dolphins or flock of Canada geese rather than bull your way through this crowded planet like a herd of angry water buffalo. With this approach, you can sail through our crazy world without receiving or inflicting scars and everyone will be happier for it.

I should sell bumper stickers. Ha ha.

So here I am lost on the highway to Los Gatos trying to find the doctor's office and I start to panic until I remind myself of my motto (which I have to do all the time – I'm no saint, believe me) and I call the office on my cell.

The woman who answers describes her surroundings and they are nothing at all like the hills and trees and houses I'm driving by. I occasionally catch an address and when I'm king there will be an address clearly placed on every house and building in the land – one of my "10 and Only 10 Laws" (sound familiar?).

The few addresses I do see are at least five digits long, making them look more like the zip codes of famous math professors.

Then I spot a place to make a U-turn and head back the way I came. I finally reach I-85 again, enter the broad slab of asphalt and concrete, and go north on the highway until I can get off and re-enter to try going south again.

Once I do, I follow my original directions but this time I go left on Winchester, curving back toward the thick band of civilization. I look out the window through my aging prescription Maui Jim sunglasses and – right there in front of me – are the buildings and other surroundings the receptionist had described about 20 minutes ago.

I find a parking space within a 10K race of the entrance, walk inside and check in at the front desk, only 25 minutes late for my 11:30 a.m. appointment.

As I wait for the doctor, I wonder what she wants to tell me and why she couldn't have done it over the phone. I've known this woman for about five months now, ever since I came down with this nasty thing called "cryptogenic organizing pneumonia (COP)" in January 2014. The more colorful phrase pulmonologists like to use is "bronchiolitis obliterans with organizing pneumonia," or BOOP.

Whether I had a case of COP or a bout of BOOP, I started having a high fever along with severe shortness of breath (taking as few as a dozen steps left me breathless). It was odd because I've never smoked tobacco – except for a couple of packs of Tareytons when I was 13. I did smoke marijuana in my college years and until my mid-30s. By then all my friends had quit so I gradually did, too, and that was a very long time ago.

To cure this rare pneumonia, the doctor put me on high doses of Prednisone (starting at 60 mg. daily). Prednisone is a hydrocortisone steroid (not the muscle-building stuff) that makes you feel and act like an NFL defensive lineman who IS on the muscle-building stuff. It brings any hidden RAGE you have in your personality to the surface, which makes you just an enormous pain in the assignation to the people in your life.

Prednisone makes you sweat like a rainforest and gain 25 pounds of water weight within a couple of months. It also swells your cheeks and other parts of your face so badly that when you enter a roomful of people, you look like you have a full moon sitting on your shoulders.

I recovered over three or four months and had a subsequent lung infection that antibiotics cleared up. So after living for more than 60 years without one, I finally had a pulmonologist among my caregivers.

About five months after our initial meeting, the doctor noticed a cloud under one of my lungs on an x-ray. She said this indicated a small pool of fluid beneath the lung. To ensure it was nothing major, she asked me to undergo an extremely painful procedure. It involved another doctor piercing my back several inches with a needle the size of a narwhal tusk to draw out the fluid.

If he had asked me to rate the pain on a 1 to 10 scale with 10 being the highest, I would have shoved the scale right up his nose.

Five days later, I sat shivering in a chair in her examination room. She had kept me waiting about 15 minutes when I heard a knock at the door. It opened and my petite pulmonologist and her thick wavy-brown hair entered the room.

After we exchanged greetings, she sat in a large leather chair behind a laminated desk. The size of the chair and her small body made her look like a bespectacled baseball in a catcher's mitt. She smiled wanly and turned until her eyes met mine. I did not care for the coldly professional look on her face.

"The best way to handle situations like this is to come right out and say it," she began. "Mr. Price (where did this formality come from? It had always been 'David' before), the analysis of the fluid in your lungs shows that you have end-stage, metastasized cancer. We found adenocarcinoma cells in your lungs, which means the cancer has spread from other parts of your body. The prognosis is not good."

I sat motionless in the examination chair. My expression undoubtedly looked like one of Rodin's *Burghers of Calais* – the one who'd just been hit in the face with a snow shovel.

"End-stage?" I said to myself. "What happened to first stage, second stage, third stage, ninety-seventh stage?"

There is no history of cancer in my family. Alzheimer's, sure, but no cancer. None of my relatives has ever had anything like this. Turns out that it's not genetic. Nobody knows why I got it. Just luck of the draw, I guess.

I have no idea what else she said. Something about only a month or two to live, more tests to pinpoint the cancer, get your things and go check into the hospital.

I do remember one thing clearly as I drove myself home. I prayed to the Higher Power I have learned to trust, rely on and treasure over the past 10 years. And this is what I said:

"Please, God, whatever you do, please, please, please don't make it pancreatic cancer."

I've known too many people who have lost loved ones to that pernicious form of the disease.

By the end of my four-day stay in the hospital, it became clear that my Higher Power had not let me down: I did not have pancreatic cancer.

I had something much worse.

By now, I had an oncologist, another specialist I never expected to need, and she informed me that what I have is cholangiocarcinoma, a quite rare form of cancer that originates in the bile ducts, which are the tubes that carry the nasty-but-necessary bile from the liver to the small intestines to aid with digestion.

She explained that I had a large tumor in my liver, anoth15er in my pancreas and a mass of sludge in the duct itself where the cancer originated. Some of the more adventurous cancer cells had already shouted "Cowabunga!" and leaped off the edge of their tumors. They splashed into the blood rushing by and dogpaddled their way to my lungs, where they homesteaded to start their own little tumors.

I learned all this shortly after I published my first novel, *Slugger*, in May 2014. I had preferred to start another novel, but decided I'd better compile a collection of my favorite shorter articles — while I had time.

I started chemotherapy shortly after the diagnosis, on June 13, 2014. The good news is that my body has responded well to a combination of western medicine and the power of multi-denominational prayer. I have great friends all over the world who are pulling for me in their own way and it's working almost miraculously. To date, all of my tumors have shrunk and the ones in my lungs have shrunk "markedly," to use doctor language.

I felt so good that on October 4, 2014 – after three wild weeks of planning and preparation (thank you for all your help, Mary Lou Simmermacher, Mary Sheehan and Erin Knight, among others) – I married Fátima, my Brazilian girlfriend who came up to be with me as soon as she heard the cancer news. For a guy who was supposed to be dead by the end of July 2014, I'm doing just fine, thank you. I'm active, productive and don't plan on dying today, which is the only thing that matters, and we're already well into 2015. Who knows?

Meanwhile, here are many of the little stories I've wrestled out of my brain – like giving birth to bucking broncos – over a 40-year career in employee communications, freelance writing and that mystical state known as "my spare time."

I added a note at the beginning of each article – except for the self-explanatory Prologue and Epilogue – that explains when I wrote it and what I was doing at the time.

I wish you and your family all the best and hope you enjoy this book.

David L. Price
January 2015

Note: This article first appeared in Tieline East, a 16-page magazine sent to employees of Hewlett-Packard's Eastern Sales Region, which was headquartered in Rockville, Maryland. We published the magazine from 1987-1991 and this article comes from the Winter 1990 edition.

It was inspired by the news that two scientists had discovered a way to use "cold fusion" to unleash massive amounts of energy in a bucket of seawater.

Playing the Palladium

I'm rapidly coming to the conclusion that everything they told us in high school was wrong – except what they said about Alcy Grimes. And they weren't completely right about *her* either.

Remember protons, neutrons and electrons? They were the Big Three of the Atom when I was driving my hormones through high school. Where are they now? Hunched over someplace where the music is sad and the beer is cheap, remembering when. They've been muscled out of their exclusive turf by quarks and quirks and photons and muons and the like.

When I was in high school an atom was something reliable – a quiet, orderly place where a few respectable particles could put in their eight hours and go home for the night.

But now? Now all helium is breaking loose. Two gentlemen with IQs that would make good bowling scores claim that nuclear fusion – the combining of two light atoms into a heavier one accompanied by the release of massive amounts of energy – can be done on a tabletop in a bucket of seawater.

Martin Fleischmann of England's University of Southhampton and B. Stanley Pons of the University of Utah knocked the scientific community onto its Periodic Table with their announcement of what they call "cold fusion." Of course, as soon as their colleagues picked themselves up off their astatine, the pointy-nosed sniping began. But apparently researchers at Stanford University have now duplicated tabletop fusion in a controlled experiment, setting off a mad scramble to find a way to harness this seemingly cheap and safe method of producing vast quantities of energy.

Before we delve into the details, a mild disclaimer must be issued. Physics has never been one of the stronger suits of this particular scribe. You're dealing with someone who thought Elementary Physics was something they taught in third grade. Or that the central question behind the Theory of Relativity was whether Uncle Hal would be able to fit on the pull-out sofa so he could sleep it off. But since I'm the only guide who isn't on break, let's form a nice straight line and plunge boldly ahead.

The keys to tabletop fusion are a silvery metal called palladium and a form of hydrogen called deuterium. For us laypeople, deuterium is hydrogen that hasn't been able to shed the 10 pounds it gained over Christmas break. It's referred to in the physics trade as "heavy hydrogen."

Deuterium has twice the mass of regular hydrogen and is readily found in seawater, which is yet another reason to head for the mountains this summer instead of the beach.

Palladium attracts deuterium atoms as powerfully as a freshly dry-cleaned suit attracts cat hair. When palladium is placed in seawater, the deuterium atoms go wild, packing themselves into the palladium latticework like college students into a Fort Lauderdale hotel room. Eventually, the place gets so crowded that the deuterium nuclei fuse, releasing tremendous amounts of energy. Again, the college-student analogy holds true.

Nobody is really sure why this happens, but a whole lot of people are staying up past the late-night talk shows trying to find out. If the theories of Fleischmann and Pons translate into practical applications, we could end up with an enormous supply of fuel without generating radioactive waste and harmful greenhouse gases.

Better still, it's so simple that anyone with a bucket of seawater, a chunk of palladium and a few "D" batteries could crank up enough juice to keep every bug zapper in the county running for months, which is big news for places like the East Coast in the summer time.

Who knows? If things go well, tabletop fusion could replace "Pictionary" or "Boggle" as the game of choice for an evening's entertainment. Phone calls such as this will take place most Friday nights: "Hey, Honey, the Barkers are coming over. Will you pick up some palladium on your way home?"

They didn't tell us any of this in high school. Back then, the atom was as boring as boron, as reliable as rhenium. It makes me wonder what they told Einstein when *he* was in high school. I'll bet they didn't know squat about the atom back then. And I know it's strange but I wonder something else. I wonder what they told him about Alcy.

Note: *Another offering from Tieline East, appearing in spring 1989. This column spawned the phrase that still makes both me and my dear friend AFPC laugh out loud: elbow hockey. You may have had to be there. AFPC, from the Eastern side of the U.S. of A., is such a great guy that he needs four letters for his initials.*

Kitchen Caboodle

It was a modest wish. My wife and I wanted to remodel our kitchen so two moderately proportioned individuals could actually stand in the room at the same time without playing elbow hockey.

It wasn't much to ask. The place our major appliances call home is a cramped 8.5 feet square, roughly the size of Donald Trump's glove compartment.

Our first clue that the project was going to be as much fun as watching underwater knitting came early on. After reciting our wish list to a highly recommended kitchen specialist (and building a fully functional model of the Great Pyramid of Cheops with sample counter tiles), we received his bid in the mail. He wanted about $45,000. In this lifetime, too.

I laughed so hard that now we have drool stains on the kitchen floor. He said he could get them out for an additional twenty grand.

Instead of giving up and spending the rest of our mornings at Mickey D's Breakfast Bar like normal people, we plunged foolishly ahead.

Two hundred phone calls and nine weekends later, we found a contractor willing to return our calls within the same calendar year. And he gave us a reasonable offer to boot. New kitchen, here we come!

Meanwhile, we had to replace the kitchen window. It's a screen-less, casement type built before the Revolutionary War and saved in case somebody needed a house built around it in Arlington, Virginia, in 1941. Its insulation value is RU-kidding, placing it just above chicken wire but slightly below a wet sweater. In the winter when I wait for my toast to pop up, my teeth chatter "The Flight of the Bumblebees" while I dance a furious flamenco in my Ninja Turtle pajamas.

Although reluctant to deprive our backyard neighbors of this highly amusing art form, we knew something had to be done.

Stupidly falling for an ancient marketing ploy known as a newspaper ad, we called the place where America shops and had a trained salesperson visit us in the convenience of our very own home. She measured the window, showed us brochures and took our order for a Supersash replacement window. We'll have it installed in six to eight weeks she promised cheerfully and then proceeded on her merry way.

A word to the uninitiated: "six to eight weeks" is a catch phrase in the home remodeling business. It means exactly the same thing as the famous dating line, "I'll call you tomorrow."

Ask a salesperson just about anything and they are programmed to give that phrase in response.

"Hey, buddy, how's the family?"

"Six to eight weeks," he will reply.

"Listen, pal, when do you think the sun's gonna burn out?"

"Six to eight weeks," he will say with a smile.

So I waited six weeks. Nothing. Eight weeks. Nothing. My suspicions aroused, I called to see how the Supersash was coming along. A painful silence followed my inquiry.

"Um, Mr. Price, let me call you back this afternoon."

That seemed promising. She could have said six to eight weeks.

The next day the phone rang.

"I have some bad news," she said. "We had another order from a Mr. Price and he canceled. Apparently someone must have pulled your order, too."

Terrific.

"So what do we do now?" asked the naïve homeowner, leading with his chin.

She suggested we place the order again. This time, however, she swore she would keep a close eye on it and do everything she could to rush it through as quickly as humanly possible.

"I guess we don't have much choice," I said. "How long do you think that will take?"

"Six to eight weeks."

So I fired her. Mild-mannered little me. It was either that or mail her a large haddock parcel post. By the time that baby got to her, revenge would be mine.

We tried another company. They promised installation in a breezy four to five weeks. Ah, progress. Then their salesperson failed to show for a crack-of-dawn measuring session. Forgot to write it down, he claimed.

I mailed him a haddock.

So here I sit, in the middle of our tiny, freezing kitchen, waiting for morning and another round of Elbow Mania. As I look out the casement window watching for the sun, I wonder what the penalty is for sending a haddock through the U.S. mail. The way my luck has been running, the judge will slam down his gavel and give me the maximum.

Six to eight weeks.

Note: *Every story I write is based on events that happened to me as filtered through the odd synaptic maze of my brain. Long ago, when I was 20, I started an assistant teaching job in an elementary school in Aurora, Colorado. There were 25 third-grade children in the class I helped with and one of them had a similar thumb unique-ability to mine. Who wouldn't want to make him feel better about it?*

My Three Thumbs

In the maternity ward of a city hospital in Camden, New Jersey, a nurse handed my mother a blue-blanketed baby. The 24-year-old woman – with her damp hair brushed back and those sweet, timid brown eyes – hugged me to her chest. She cradled me securely with her left arm and explored this new prize – her second son – with her right. She stroked my cheek, my neck and my shoulder. Down my arm she went, past the crook of my little elbow, my forearm and my tiny right hand.

She felt my fingers as my hand reflexively grabbed at hers. One, two, three, she counted, breathing slowly, exhausted from the lack of sleep and the physical exertion. Four, five, six.

Six? Wait a minute. That can't be right. Let's try it again. One, two, three, four, five, SIX!

"Nurse!"

Somehow the attendants in the delivery room missed a little something. But you'll never slip an extra thumb past a mother. Technically, it's called thumb polydactylism, one of the most common birth defects affecting the hand. One online medical site claims that one out of every 500 babies is born with some form of polydactylism, from a small stub of soft tissue to a fully formed thumb or finger. It is believed to be genetic and carried down from generation to generation.

When my former embryonic self was a mere 15 days old, one of the tiny tissue buds that would become my fingers split. Eventually that split turned into my extra thumb. My family talked of a great uncle in Wales who had the same condition, except he kept his. I imagine people were startled when he shook hands with them and he wrapped that extra thumb around their fingers.

Oh, imagine the things you could do with an extra digit! You could become an accomplished pianist with a rollicking, boogie-woogie style that would put Jerry Lee Lewis to shame. Or a professional baseball pitcher! You could sling a three-seam fastball that rose, dipped and darted to the side – nastier than Mariano Rivera's splitter.

Alas, my parents kept me from the life of a great entertainer, athlete or circus freak by asking the hospital's pediatric surgeon to remove my bonus gift. Much later, my mother told me how she had fretted over the decision. She said it wasn't fair to make such a difficult choice without knowing what I would have wanted.

I told her it was fine. It is what it is. If people are curious, I'll explain my prodigious digits. I'll show them my left and right thumbs side by side so they can see how the right one is nearly half the size of the left – like a Mini-me brother. The right one is also almost wrinkle-free, since I have quite limited motion with the upper joint.

Then I'll spread my fingers as wide as they go and place my hands together, palms touching. This way people can see that my right thumb splits the difference between where my normal left thumb and index finger are.

I also tell them it's no big deal. I'm right-handed and I pitched in organized youth baseball leagues through 9th grade and even threw a two-hitter once. (The first hit I gave up was a cheap single. The second was a moon shot to right field that went as high and far as the Neptune probe – you could have eaten three dozen Memphis-style barbecued ribs and still had time to wet-nap your face and hands before that baby came back to earth.)

I also play guitar and juggle (not at the same time). I admit I'm no threat to Eric Clapton, Slash or Cirque de Soleil, but I'm not awful either. The point is that I've never fretted about my disability.

Twenty years after my appearance on this earth at that hospital in Camden, my two remaining thumbs and I got a job as a teaching assistant at an elementary school in Aurora, Colorado. My main responsibility was to help the teacher, Mrs. Warren, ride herd on 30 or so 3rd and 4th Grade kids in an experimental teaching program.

For the most part, the school had open classrooms where the children had limited structure, even at an early age. The kids who couldn't cope with that and needed a more rigid structure were assigned to my class, which resembled a traditional school room.

One day all the kids but one were outside at lunch recess, running like dogs. Cal – who was one of the fit, athletic kids –

stayed behind. He sat at his desk with his head down, resting on his arms.

I asked Mrs. Warren what was wrong with him.

"He's upset about his thumbs," she told me.

"His thumbs?" I asked.

She told me that Cal was born missing a thumb on his left hand and with an extra one on his right. He'd had the extra thumb removed shortly after birth, just like I had. On some days, being different from the other kids makes him sad, Mrs. Warren said. And sometimes they tease him about it. Today was one of his sad days.

I briefly told her my story and she asked if I would go share it with him. Of course, I said.

So I walked over to Cal and asked if I could talk to him. He nodded softly. So I told him about my hand, showed him the difference between my right and left thumbs. I let him see the scars on my wrist where they removed part of the extra tendon and attached it to my baby thumb to try to give it more mobility in the top joint. I let him trace the pale scars that snaked across the base of my thumb, the ones from the operation I'd had at 14 to take away the bump left from my initial surgery at five days old.

Then I told Cal that none of it mattered. I said that I'd pitched in Little League, I play guitar. I shared my family's story about my great uncle in Wales who had kept his third thumb.

And we laughed. We were two freaks of nature, different from the others and with an immediate and special bond because of it. After we finished talking, Cal got up and ran outside to play.

Later that day, when the kids were engrossed in a project, Mrs. Warren called me over. I anticipated her thanking me, telling me what an inspiration I was to Cal. Thanks to our talk, she was going to say, I was his new idol and the boy was ready to think positively and move on with his life.

"I spoke to Cal," she told me. "You know what he said?"

"No," I replied, eager to hear the praise that was coming my way.

"He said: 'Mr. Price's thumb is even uglier than mine!'"

"Oh," I replied, the hot flash of embarrassment reddening my cheeks. Oh, my.

I was certain she could hear my ego deflating, but she didn't let on. So I just smiled.

At the end of the school day, I watched Cal get up from his desk and gather his things. He seemed like just another happy kid. As he walked out the door, I remember thinking, "Good for you, Cal. Good for you.

"Three thumbs up, my little friend. Three thumbs up."

Note: *Following is one of my most commercially successful little stories. This article was published both in "Hemispheres," the in-air flight magazine from United Airlines, as well as MEASURE, the global Hewlett-Packard magazine published by the genial and inimitable Jay Coleman. The article hit the friendly skies in the late 1990s.*

Hail to the Sheets

Late in the evening of a business day that started at dawn in Salt Lake City, I staggered into the lobby of a popular hotel chain about a mile from the San Francisco airport. I was loaded down like a prospector's mule with a bloated garment bag and a briefcase that would have been lighter had it been filled with bars of plutonium.

I dropped the bag on the shiny linoleum floor by the check-in sign, slung my briefcase onto the counter and stated my name to a perky young woman with a gold badge that announced her to the world as "Merissa."

She smiled sweetly and her fingers pounced onto her computer keyboard, making it clack with that urgent staccato rhythm. She stared for a moment. She clacked again. More staring. More clacking. More staring. Then she turned to me with a practiced look of dismay on her face and pronounced the six words that can dash the spirit of even the most seasoned business traveler.

"Do you have a confirmation number?"

Momentarily rattled, I opened my briefcase and shuffled through the contents. I knew full well that the magic phrase to open Aladdin's Cave was nowhere inside my leather carryall and that I had made the unforgivable sin of trusting the people who booked my travel reservations.

"Is this it?" I bluffed, showing her a number scrawled on a piece of note paper.

"No," sniffed the guardian of the gates. "Ours begin with a letter."

She didn't even reveal which one. She was good.

"I'm sorry," Merissa said, "but we're full tonight. I can't take you without a confirmation number."

"But what am I supposed to do?" I countered, hoping pathos would get me further than fury. "Someone made the reservation here. They just didn't give me the number."

"I'll have to talk to my manager," she said.

Merissa turned briskly and disappeared through the doorway behind the counter. I stood there alone, muttering creative combinations of words I'd learned as an adolescent. Several minutes crept by like an elephant seal with a pulled hamstring.

Though exhausted, disheveled and beginning to be disconsolate, I retained a flicker of hope. I knew fair Merissa was fighting the good fight behind that closed door, arguing for compassion in the face of cold bureaucracy.

The coherent side of my brain knew better. A few synapses were still awake over there, crackling like cold tap water poured into a frying pan fresh off the stove. Merissa was no doubt sitting behind that wall with her feet up, smoking a Camel No. 9, catching up on Twitter and laughing at my predicament.

I stared at the life-sized portrait of an obviously important man on the wall behind the counter. He had a smile that snickered, "Our profits were up 23 percent last quarter."

This guy didn't give a rat's pancreas about me or my confirmation number.

Merissa burst back through the door. Was it my imagination or could I really smell smoke?

"My manager says we can't take you without a confirmation number," she chirped.

As an option, fury was looking better and better.

"Look," I started, my Y chromosomes leaping out of their beds, sliding down the pole and hopping into their boots. "I stay in your hotels all the time. My company spends a lot of money with you. A reservation was made for me. Somehow it didn't get through. I'm in a strange city. I have no place to sleep. What am I supposed to do?"

"Well," said Merissa, apparently swayed by my measured control of my temper, "we could put you in the Presidential Suite."

Ah. Okay. Now you're talking, Merissa. The Presidential Suite! Think of it: a spacious room, tasteful Early American furniture, bronze eagles on the headboard, a Mount Rushmore Jacuzzi with water jetting out of Teddy Roosevelt's nose.

Of course, it might cost a bit more. But, heck, it was all they had! Surely those giddy pranksters in accounting would understand.

"Now, it doesn't have a bed," she said, yanking me from my reverie. "But we could bring in a cot."

"No bed?"

"It does have a sink and a toilet," she continued. "But there's no shower."

"No bed? No shower?"

"That's right."

"In the Presidential Suite? President of what, Berzerkistan?"

"I'm sorry, sir, but that's the best we can do."

In defense of our nation's leader, nay, in response to the most callous marketing ploy I had yet to discover, I launched a furious, patriotic attack.

"How dare you insult the president of the United States," I shouted. "Who do you think you are, professional athletes?"

Merissa was unmoved. She did, however, call a nearby hotel. She chatted amiably with someone on the telephone, hung up and informed me that she'd made a reservation for me at a place only a mile away.

Defeated, I thanked her for this small gesture, gathered my tonnage and shuffled out. I hefted my bags into the rental car and steered the metallic camel to the next oasis. It would be my fourth hotel in three cities in three nights.

It marked the final outpost in a trip shrouded with the standard travel woes: mysteriously missing confirmation numbers; flu-ridden fellow travelers sneezing in my general direction in airports and on flights; lousy sleep on pillows that were either as thin as a napkin or as unyielding as a cinder block; plus, insolent clerks and cramped quarters. Ah, the glamour of business travel!

I pulled into the parking lot of the next hotel, lugged my belongings and plodded into a cavernous lobby flecked with hints of the Southwest. I announced my presence to the efficient-looking young man behind the counter. He clacked away merrily at his computer for a moment. Then he frowned with that same look a car mechanic gives you when he's about to tell you that your brake pads are shot and he'd better replace all four of them before you drive your car another inch.

"Excuse me, sir," he said, "do you have a confirmation number?"

Oh, no. Merissa. You siren. You drew me near with your alluring song only to laugh as my boat crashed into the rocky shoals. You got me, Merissa. You got me good.

I had to think fast or get far more acquainted with the streets of San Francisco than I ever wanted to be.

"Look," I said, in my most imperial tone. "I cannot believe you do not recognize me. I am president of Berzerkistan. Take me to my suite."

Note: *He's published! At the callow age of 23 (a prime number!), "Denver" magazine, which served my hometown of Englewood, Colorado, decided to take a chance on a young writer and accepted the following humor article for publication.*

As a prime example of "write what you know," it's a satire of the restaurant service trade, which means I was still bouncing back and forth between living at home and having my very own utility bills, which I paid by waiting table until I could find something better. The edition that included this article hit the newsstands in summer 1978. This is the unedited version.

Sorry, No Substitutions

Most scholars accept the year 2037 B.C. as the founding date of modern technique in culinary service. Those few dissenters have had their grants revoked and are now dutifully cleaning the dolphin tanks, so we can be certain of the general acceptability of this fact.

In that year, deep in the mountainous countryside of Gaelic Wales, a historic event took place that would startle the as-yet-uncivilized world. The unlikely protagonist was a grizzled, ancient Welshman answering to the name of Gaelen Llewellyn. Gaelen continued a proud tradition just as his father and his father's father had: He was a waiter.

During the evening in question, Gaelen was serving the local chieftain and his council of elders. The meal had been finished, with the guests settling down with a mug of locally brewed mead to pop corn over the fire and discuss the pros and cons of learning how to write.

In those days, a man waited table because he was ordered to and most found it disadvantageous to argue, with health plans as primitive as they were at the time. Tips were non-existent; complaints over schedules were settled with a quick mallet blow to the instep; and conditions were bad enough to give an OSHA inspector night sweats. Gaelen Llewellyn was about to change it all.

He had already been attributed with several innovations in the field of food service. Gaelen was the first to utter that cryptic legend, "Sorry, no substitutions," when an elder whined about the vegetable. Also, on a very dark night, his failing eyesight forced him to say, "Okay, who had the elk salad?" (This has been misquoted over recent years, but eyewitness accounts assure us that "elk" is indeed the proper translation.)

But that memorable night with the chieftain and the elders was to be the zenith of the old man's career. He had spent the better part of the afternoon quaffing mead and trying unsuccessfully to juggle three small rocks – a highly regarded pastime in ancient circles. Apparently, Gaelen continued drinking well into the evening, suggesting his condition by giggling whenever anyone asked about the "plat du jour." He was fondling his oats to such an extent that he decided he was owed some compensation for the excellent service he was providing. After all, he had changed the ash trays twice and told several amusing anecdotes between courses, hadn't he?

Gaelen stumbled over to the chief, who was telling Etruscan jokes and yanked his wild boar-skin coat out from under him. The maneuver caught the chief by surprise and he rolled into the fire, much to the delight of his companions who were roundly amused by this unusual act.

"Gratuity," mumbled Gaelen. "Thanks very much."

Historians differ as to what happened next. Some argue that the chief had Gaelen filled with a molten substance that inspired the expression "Bronze Age." Others mention the phrase "chopped into mincemeat" in connection with the incident. A few radical scholars have even suggested that the chief laughed off the whole affair in a boys-will-be-boys manner and allowed Gaelen to marry his daughter Rayena, who had the Face That Sank Three Log Canoes.

Whatever became of Gaelen was inconsequential to anyone other than his next of kin and local florists, but a trend had been set. No longer would those of the waiting persuasion be forced to subject themselves to the grossest of indignations with no means of recall. In short, Gaelen Llewellyn first suggested the most essential facet for a waiter's psychological well-being: Revenge!

Over the centuries, the problems in dealing with the unruly general public have changed. For instance, in Roman times, waiters had to put up with drunken legionnaires singing dirty limericks about young men from Pompeii and doing spirited impersonations of Edith Hamilton. Today, the abuse is more psychological in nature.

A case in point is the ubiquitous party of 24 plump matrons demanding separate checks and no ice in their Diet Cokes. It's little consolation that they will all order the spinach salad with bleu cheese dressing (except for the few radical women who will ask for balsamic vinaigrette). And it is indeed exciting to hunt for the dimes and quarters quaintly stashed beneath napkins, salt shakers, bread plates and all the other fun hiding places, but the situation is fraught with abuse for the poor waiting class.

But due to a seemingly insignificant historical incident more than three thousand years ago, the modern waiter can tilt his bow tie to a jaunty angle or straighten the name tag on her blouse and approach the table with confidence. At last, for every elbow caught in the midsection while grinding pepper, for every obnoxious devil in a three-piece suit who snaps his fingers and calls you "Boy," for every plate one must distastefully scrape the remains from, for every act of disdain, for every separate check, and, yes, even for every doggy bag – there are means of reprisal.

All wait people learn the procedures for vengeance early in their career as a means to lash out against cruelty, injustice, vanity and downright rude behavior. These equalizers are passed down from waiter to trainee these days – rather than father to son – since the lifespan of restaurant personnel is shorter than that of an asthmatic glass blower. It is even rumored that every person of the waiting persuasion carries a leather-bound copy of the seminal book called "Quotations from Gaelen Llewellyn: Ten Ways to Turn the Tables."

Whether this is true is sheer speculation, but if you ever see your waiter in a darkened corner thumbing through a dog-eared manual with an evil glint in his eyes, prepare yourself for one of the following.

Bombs over Winnetka. Highly effective in dealing with mild annoyances, this technique involves dropping an entrée onto the table from a distance of eighteen inches to three feet above the target. The distance depends on the length of your arms and the resiliency of the china involved. Broken plates are effective, but management can always demonstrate its displeasure by either making not-so-subtle adjustments to your paycheck or siccing the guard dog on you after hours.

The resounding clatter will be annoying for your patrons at the very least. Be sure to accompany the disturbance with a sardonic smile and the pronouncement: "Oh, I am so sorry," being certain to put the emphasis on the "so."

Remember, beginners, under no circumstances are you to clean up anything knocked over during the encounter. It tends to weaken the effect and, after all, this manual is meant for wait persons not busboys, who have their own means of reprisal.

The Hollandaise Shuffle. Although named after the sauce employed in the original incident, any creamy, staining or scalding substance can be used. This technique was initially mastered by Parisian waiters since the French would dump a sauce on even fruit salad if not forcefully restrained.

Availability and unmitigated gall are the essentials in the Hollandaise Shuffle. Since the procedure is simple enough, many waiters use the technique though few are proficient enough to achieve the honorary title, Grandmaster of Slop – which is often awarded posthumously if the victim is the member of a professional sporting team.

With this technique, it is not sufficient to merely "spill" the sauce. A true professional will act out his moment like Olivier doing Hamlet or Fey doing Sarah Palin. Be sure to approach the offending person with extreme insouciance, even going so far as to hum some endearing folk ballad such as "Jimmy Crack Corn" or "She'll Be Comin' 'Round the Mountain." Your target will either be soothed into relaxation or filled with wonder as to what the hell's gotten into you. At any rate, it will shut him or her up, giving you complete control of the situation.

Out of the corner of your eye, spot a busboy hurrying by and wait until he's almost upon you and feign a collision as you are pouring sauce onto your target's dinner. The resulting impact should seem like enough to excuse the pouring of a gooseneck filled with your chosen weapon down the entire front of an expensive Italian suit or milady's original, supremely expensive creation. To further eliminate blame and/or physical violence, swear profusely in a language other than English (French or Spanish are adequate, but Afghani or Mandarin are strokes of genius).

For those of you who speak foreign tongues as mellifluously as a garbage disposal crammed with watermelon rind and chicken bones, simply look aghast and mutter, "Oh, dear, dear me." Emphasis, of course, on the latter "dear." And remember, when called upon to help mop up, always smear, never dab.

The Harry Houdini. If a diner is exceptionally unruly or troublesome, more urgent means are required. In such a case, one must recall the cardinal rule of waiting table: They can't get served without you. When that loudmouthed Bozo really fries your cupcakes, control your desire to drown him in a tub of Tejava iced tea and simply disappear. Obviously, it's more entertaining if you can perform this feat with a cloud of smoke while clearing the salads, but sneaking off before the entrée is served to read some of the more involved passages of Dostoevsky in the employee rest room will suffice.

The Hallelujah, Bound for Glory. If all else fails and your need for revenge is yet to be gratified, this is your baby. Never, I repeat, never, has this technique failed. The results are often devastating: Several professional diners have been spotted on street corners eating cold Spam from the can with plastic spoons while reciting obscure Old French vowels after exposure to the Hallelujah, Bound for Glory. So, please, wait people, use your discretion.

The vehicle in this case is a seemingly innocent flambé. Wheel the cart up to the table with a good-natured smile, exposing as many pearly whites as good taste allows. Prepare the dish slowly (Note: Steak au poivre is recommended for beginners, rack of lamb for the intermediate and Crepes Suzette for those truly accomplished professionals). (Additional note: If the party in question was rude enough not to order a dish that is normally flambéed, either borrow an entrée from an understanding compatriot or go ahead and flame whatever's there. After all, what the hell do they know, anyhow? You're the one in control.

Now, light the burner with suitable flair and place the pan upon it. Here's the trick: Create a diversion that catches the attention of your patrons. This can be done either by prearranging for the cocktail waitress to saunter by in a dress revealing as much cleavage as is acceptable under local blue laws or by releasing a moderately sized rodent on the next occupied table. (Screams are sure-fire attention-getters.)

If the cocktail waitress causes an embarrassing scene upon your request for a more overt display of bosom by phoning her husband, the mixed martial arts champion, or you happen to have an irrational fear of small animals to the point of actually shrieking in ascending order the list of words banned for television broadcast whenever you're within 10 feet of one, hope still springs eternal. Most everyone assumes no one falls for the hackneyed gag, "Quick, look at the moose!" But don't let them kid you – it still works like a charm.

When no one is looking, pour the entire bottle of 151-proof rum into the pan and tilt it slightly so some of the rum hits the flame. The resulting explosion will be talked about for years to come. Personal damage is typically limited to secondary sex characteristic like goatees and eyebrows since the fire usually blows itself out almost as quickly as it catches, but what an effect! Some even say that the image of a waiter leaping out in front of a backdrop of mushrooming flame inspired Felicia Hemans to write her poem about that brave lad on the burning deck.

Incidentally, those wait persons brassy enough to vie for a sparkling combination of insult and injury will return to the table a few moments later and innocently ask, "Will there be anything else this evening?"

Abnormal Approaches. In this, the Chinese Year of the Social Deviant, there are those with a penchant for the bizarre. Quite often they end up in restaurants for various reasons including free food, odd hours, easily accessible matches and those adorable uniforms. The following are methods of retribution that most people in the restaurant trade consider tacky beyond belief and rarely contemplate using them, but we should all be aware of their existence.

A. Infectious Disease. Malaria is an ever-popular favorite in this category, but tracking down an appropriately infected mosquito can be tedious and proper presentation of the insect is always a bother: Is garnish enough? Should a vegetable be included? You see the problem.

Plague can be a viable alternative, but prairie dogs have a voracious nip and it's rumored that throughout history they have never much cared for the serving class.

B. Zoological Theatrics. Serving the entrée from the back of an elephant or suitably horned ungulate is guaranteed to raise a few titters from even the most refined diners. Unfortunately, zoning commissioners are known to have a strict interpretation of local codes and the night cleaning crew would have their hands full, quite literally.

While an anaconda peeking out from beneath an apron or a phalanx of trained army ants is great for laughs, good taste prohibits their use, with Mother's Day and Christmas as the only notable exceptions.

Undoubtedly, there are other tantalizing schemes that could be added to a wait person's arsenal, but few have proved as useful and soul-satisfying as the one's mentioned above. There will always be radical groups promoting less subtle means, but try not to become helplessly entangled in their web of the obvious. Remember, if these tactics are not observed with at least a modicum of savoir faire, you'll end up in more trouble than a Gothic architect with fallen arches.

So go forth, you of the serving class, with heads unbowed and cocktail trays uplifted, and shout the words of the great blind poet John Milton. Yes, when he wrote, "They also serve who only stand and wait," he was referring, of course, to you.

Note: *This one stemmed from my frustration with online dating sites after I was divorced in 2005. In my experience, there are two things an adult man or woman never wants to do after the age of 45: look for a new job or date. I've had to do both and the online experience is not for me. I wrote this in the spring of 2009.*

Naked Lips and All

With apologies to Aesop, I'm going to tell you the moral at the beginning: Never, ever use your face to lie. Ignore this warning and your retribution will be swift, humiliating and far worse than something as simple and trivial as dying.

I moved recently, which is an opportunity to sift through all the detritus you've accumulated over a lifetime of living. While sorting through your dusty cache of letters, souvenirs and badges of honor, you'll find all kinds of interesting tidbits, including pictures from back in the day when a BlackBerry only stained your fingers.

After looking at photos stretched over a few decades, I realized something that in hindsight should have been obvious: Throughout most of my adulthood, I've sported some form of facial hair.

Post college, it was a thick black moustache that would have given Nietzsche a nervous tic. In my early years working at a famous computer and printer company — and patrolling left field for the 39ers, a competitive men's softball team in Fairfax County, Virginia — I wore a full beard. And forgive me for digressing, but now that I look back, I don't think 39ers referred to a gold rush some place. More likely it was the average age of our players.

But for the past 10 years or so, I've worn what most people call a goatee. Wikipedia defines it as "A beard formed by a tuft of hair on the chin ... In recent years, goatee has come to denote a style of facial hair that connects to a moustache."

My version is the latter, with a moustache, and I keep the whole ensemble closely cropped so no Billy goats, nannies or lonely shepherds follow me down the street.

All was fine until last month when I noticed something natural but horrifying: The majority of hair on my chin had somehow managed to turn itself white. Seemingly overnight, my salt-and-pepper goatee looked like I'd gone down on a salt lick. If my chin were a bag of Fritos, I'd have a surgeon general's warning plastered across it.

For weeks, I debated whether or not to do something to hide this abominable snowman's beard. In a moment of moral ambiguity, I purchased a package of a men's facial-hair-coloring product. I hid it in a drawer in my bathroom and would peek every few days to see if it were still there.

We interrupt the chronological flow of this narrative for a relevant few words about marriage. If you've been married for a long time, you often hang on — even if it's rockier than the front side of El Capitan — for one reason and one reason only, and it's not the kids. It's because the thought of ever having to date again scares you to death.

Women to me are like a giant ATM with a huge stack of $20 bills inside. I have a card that goes in smoothly, but I have no idea what the PIN is. I keep clacking in random sequences of numbers, but no cash ever comes out. And then the machine eats my card and spits the remains onto the sidewalk.

Don't get me wrong. I have many wonderful female friends and my camaraderie with them significantly enriches my life. It's just that if love were a lake, I'm currently standing in the middle of the Bonneville Salt Flats. And there are times when I miss being in love – not just being pheromonal, mind you – but really in love, when two healthy, independent people choose to cuddle with each other.

Since we human critters are always looking for a scapegoat, I started to blame my lack of post-marriage dating success on the white in my beard. It couldn't be the fact that I'm still getting over the wounds from my divorce or that my Higher Power thinks I still have some evolving to do before trying to enter into a successful relationship. It couldn't have been that. It had to be all those tiny white hairs, standing upright and saluting.

So one night, I put some Lucinda Williams on, took out the package hidden in my bathroom drawer and set out to alter Mother Nature's handiwork.

I followed the directions carefully, first putting on the thin plastic gloves they thoughtfully included in the package. Then I squirted a thin line of what looked like loose cat poop from one tube into the mixing tray and then a line of chalky toothpaste from the other. I mixed the chemical solution together in the tray, using the hard plastic end of the application brush.

Then I cleaned off the mixing end of the brush, as directed, turned it around and dipped the sturdy bristles into the solution. I brushed the mixture into my goatee, chin first, until I had the whole thing covered. It took only three minutes by my watch – which doesn't have a second hand – and the instructions said I should keep it up for no more than five minutes. Wanting the full effect, I dipped the brush back into the glop and applied some more.

After five minutes, I stopped. I glanced briefly into the mirror and my goatee seemed to be getting darker and darker. The next step called for me to rinse off the mixture. So I turned the knob on my shower, felt the water until it was hot enough and jumped in.

Just in case these chemicals were more dangerous than advertised, I held my hands over my goolies – like male soccer players in front of a goal kick – to keep the rinsed-off solution away from those tender parts.

I finished showering, toweled off, wrapped a drier towel around my waist and stepped in front of the mirror. I grabbed a hand towel, wiped away the condensation and expected to see this handsome, dark-goateed man staring back at me.

I was shocked by my reflection. This huge, charcoal-looking smudge encircled my mouth. My face looked like a child's drawing of the tramp clown, the one with the thick five-o'clock-shadow drawn in.

The goatee was dark all right – every last hair was black. But the solution also seemed to have dyed black all the skin underneath. I looked like a middle-aged man with a Barnum-and-Bailey's fetish.

I swear if I walked down the street looking like that on any day but Halloween, people would run inside and slam their doors. I looked like a hobo criminal who escaped from the insane asylum. Try that for a Match.com description.

I walked out to the kitchen and my cat ran away and hid under the dining room table. Oh, this will have the women flocking my way. Everyone wants to date a man who looks like he drew a goatee onto his face with a charcoal briquette.

So I lathered up my face and shaved the whole thing off. My face was as naked as a mole rat, as smooth as an ice rink after the Zamboni's passed by, as soft as the nape of an alpaca's neck.

The next day, I went to a meeting at noon. The first person I saw was a close female friend and she said, "Hey, you shaved off your beard!"

"Yes," I replied.

"How come?" she asked.

"I cannot tell a lie," I said. "I've gotten an offer to play left field for the San Francisco Giants. And they don't allow facial hair."

"Oh," she replied, thinking it over. "Tried to color it, huh?"

Crap, I said to myself. Women. Sometimes they make you just want to dye.

Note: *When I first thought I was writing a compilation of articles for a book, I wrote this as the introduction. However, that first book turned out to be the novel "Slugger" instead. This article, written in summer 2012, still works at explaining how I feel about writing, so I saved it.*

I am a self-avowed nature freak who loves animals of all kinds and adores touring the Monterey Bay Aquarium or Año Nuevo or watching television shows on ocean-bound and other critters.

One day I was watching a show that included underwater footage of blue whales and I was astonished at how something so enormous can be so graceful. While I'm on the other side of the spectrum from enormous, I can be clumsy – both physically and emotionally – with my encounters on land. But it all clicks into place when I sit in front of my computer keyboard.

Cetacean Break

This is the best chance I'll ever have to explain my writing career so here goes. I've been blessed with the ability to string words together in meaningful ways and have worked hard at improving the talent I was given. I've been making a decent living doing what I was born to do since I was in my early twenties and an even better living once I shifted to corporate communications.

How many people are fortunate enough to spend their working lives doing what they love to do? I consider myself quite blessed on this front and it makes up for some of the other facets of my life where I've had considerable struggles.

On the creative side, I wrote my first short story in second grade and remember calling it, "How the Cheetah Got His Spots." I don't recall any of the details, but I do know that my teacher, Mrs. Brown, gave me an A+ and wrote "very original" on it.

I ran into her at a department store three years later and was stunned to see her outside of school. I didn't know teachers were allowed outside of school.

I adored Mrs. Brown who had short dark hair that matched her name and she might have been 50 years old or so when she taught me. I didn't care about her age because I had my first schoolboy crush. After all, she volunteered me for the male lead in the second grade play, a student version of Hansel and Gretel. My best memory of the action on stage was the part where I got to shove that snooty Anne Koontz – who played the witch – into the oven and turn her into a lump of coal. That was the highlight of my seven-year-old life to date and it was all thanks to Mrs. Brown.

Five years later, I heard the rumor that she had "put an end to herself," as people said in those days to avoid the shock and stigma associated with the word "suicide." I was sad for a long time.

Another of my stories from my seminal year with Mrs. Brown was a parody of "Jack and the Beanstalk." It went pretty much like the original, but I added a twist. While trying to escape from the Giant, Jack trips over the golden harp he was stealing and gets caught. The Giant throws him into a dungeon and the story ends with Jack staring up at the narrow slit of a window about 10 feet from the dank, concrete floor. The text went like this:

Jack looked up at the tiny window above him and thought to himself he would never get out.
And he never did.

If that doesn't sound like a kid who needs antidepressants already, I don't know what does. I was probably born with the chemical imbalance that causes depression and remember spending lots of time alone in my basement room (the rest of my family lived upstairs) either reading, studying or listening to the radio during arguably the best decade ever for popular music – the 1960s.

Everything went reasonably well in my little life until I hit adolescence. When I was 14 years old, I became quite ill and no one could figure out what was wrong. I was constantly fatigued and had ongoing outbreaks of canker sores that erupted in my tender mouth and throat all the way down into my stomach.

Here's a funny story from that time. They took me to the hospital to stay for a few days and to undergo tests. A lady doctor was interviewing me after I had eaten a hospital lunch, including a half peach in heavy sauce that I was saving for after the doctor left.

She asked me several things and then came to a question that stumped me. "What color is your stool?" she said.

First of all, I was a nervous 14-year-old boy with an illness no one could figure out and now a lady doctor was asking very personal questions. Second, I had no idea what she meant. I had never heard the word "stool" to mean anything but a four-legged, round thing you sit on.

So I told her I didn't know. But she persisted.

"Is it the color of the door (which was brown) or the color of the peach on your tray?"

Never wanting to disappoint anyone – a people-pleaser since birth – I nodded and said that, yes, my stool was the color of the peach on my tray.

So they added "yellow stool" to my growing list of complaints.

Somewhere in there they decided to give me a shot of gamma globulin to see what happened. It worked, kicking my weakened immune system back into gear and I slowly got better. Unfortunately, I ended up missing almost three months of ninth grade and the administrators gave me a deal without bothering to talk to me. They decided I could continue with my ninth grade class and they would give me straight "Cs" for the semester I missed.

Since 9th grade is the first year on your high school transcript, they gave me – otherwise an "A" student – a handicap of straight "C's." That's like putting ankle weights on a sprinter's legs and expecting him to win a 100-meter race against Usain Bolt. It triggered my lifelong, stuck-in-adolescence belief that life just isn't fair. As one of my early sponsors would say years later, "Tough shit, don't drink." It's a good motto.

Even though no one diagnosed it at the time that was my first bout with Crohn's Disease. It essentially went dormant – except for regular bouts with painful sores in my mouth and on my tongue whenever I was overwhelmed by stress – until it arrived in full force when I was 28 and had just moved to Washington, D.C., from my hometown of Englewood, Colorado.

Too much has happened since then to give it justice here. Some of the highlights: I started a career in writing shortly after graduating from college. Initially, I worked as an on-air news reporter and then as a feature and news writer for a cable television trade magazine in Denver, Colorado.

When I was 27, I took an offer from a rival publication to become their deputy bureau chief in Washington, D.C., and moved there without ever having set foot in the D.C. area. It turned out to be a fascinating beat, covering the Federal Communications Commission, Congress (Barry Goldwater, Jr. read one of my articles into the record one day on the floor of the Senate) and even a session at the Supreme Court.

In my early 30s, I realized that if I wanted to make a decent living writing, I needed to jump over to employee communications and the corporate world, which requires many of the same skills as reporting, but the pay and benefits are much better. So that's what I've done for almost 30 years now to support my wife (who is long gone, but we're finally friends again) and two wonderful children (still a huge and essential part of my life).

In addition to the corporate gig, I've made a grand total of almost $800 selling some of my short humor articles for publication in commercial magazines. Despite my success on the corporate side, there are days when I wonder what would have happened had I stayed in Denver and chosen the freelance path instead. Then I remember the great line from Satchel Paige, the immortal baseball pitcher who finally earned a cup of coffee in the Major Leagues after spending his prime segregated into the Negro Leagues: "Don't look back. Something may be gaining on you."

I started working for a major California-based company in its Rockville, Maryland, sales office in the late 1980s and was relocated with my family to Silicon Valley in the mid-1990s. I've been here ever since.

My Crohn's Disease is in remission now, as long as I take a couple of pills daily and give myself an injection in my belly every two weeks. The treatment options are much better now than they were when I first came down with the illness at 14. Incidentally, my doctors have told me repeatedly that a cure is only five years away. They have now been telling me this for 46 years.

I'm a recovering alcoholic and drug addict (prescription Vicodin to combat the pain and other symptoms of Crohn's), and I've been clean and sober for almost eight years. I've been guided through a lot of inner work, too, and can now say that I finally know how to be at peace with myself. I'm getting better at living in the moment, and reacting with kindness and understanding rather than rage.

I also met a wonderful woman online in an unusual, serendipitous manner revealed in the Epilogue to this book. She's perfect for me in so many essential ways and loves me just the way I am. The only problem? She lives in very southern Brazil, about 7,500 frequent-flier miles away. Best guess, there are more than 160 million females in America. Maybe 80 million of them are between 40 and 60 years old, but I had to go to another country to find one that doesn't mind putting up with me.

Finally, I am a classic introvert and need to be alone to recharge. Myers-Briggs has me nailed on this one.

There are days when I feel like a blue whale. Have you ever seen one up close? A blue whale's skin is marred with barnacles and other parasitic creatures, stuck like dried pasta to his sides. His body is etched with long white and gray scars, reminders of every battle he's ever had with a great white shark or giant squid or orca or even a motorboat or cruise ship.

Up close, he's a mess. He looks like a monster – the stuff of nightmares – not the romantic, story-book image we have of the ocean's monarch. But back up the camera to about 30 meters away. Watch him soar through the blue-green ocean and up to the surface where he breaches into the world of light, blows the used air from his lungs, sucks in clean and shimmering oxygen, and crashes back down into the water.

See him dive. He fans the water with his powerful tail, rhythmically pushing down, down. Then he levels off, pulling up his huge head with those wise, knowing eyes and he glides to the right slowly, rolling and twisting through the dark blue depths with the poise and grace of a prima ballerina.

It's hard to believe that such a massive creature can be so lithe, so graceful underwater. But it's absolutely true. He's beautiful when he swims.

And that's what it's like for me. I struggle through life sometimes with the physical and mental illnesses I've been given. But when I sit in front of a computer keyboard, my brain engaged and my fingers flying – the blank page before me filling up with those tiny letters so neatly arranged into little packages – I feel like a blue whale, gliding easily through the water. I feel alive. I feel free.

I feel beautiful.

Note: *My job in Hewlett-Packard's Eastern Sales Region was exciting, productive and I worked with a wonderful group of people. This article deals with my attempts to cope with Crohn's Disease with a bit of tongue-in-cheek humor, so to speak. It was published in the Winter 1992 edition of Tieline East.*

My Life with Lentils

Way back in 1980 about 18 inches of my large intestine called a wildcat strike and walked off the job, creating some serious havoc with deliverables.

It was a ridiculously stressful time in my life. I had moved away from my family and friends in the Denver area to Washington, D.C. – a city I had never even visited. I was also broke; I had a new job in the publishing business where deadline pressures were constant and intense; I was recovering from an ulcer and a hiatal hernia, both of which I was too young to have earned; and a bungled love affair had clubbed me over the head, taken my wallet and left me in a ditch by the side of the road with my hands duct-taped behind me.

My colon responded to all this by tap dancing to European thrash music for a couple of weeks. Then – filled with painful, bleeding ulcerations that had seared their way into its pale pink tissues – the organ shut itself down, leaving me with a high fever and desperately ill. And thanks to the harshest of loopholes that no one had bothered to point out ahead of time, I was two weeks short of qualifying for benefits with my new employer and therefore utterly without health insurance. Welcome to Washington!

But even the most terrible train wreck looks better from a distance. Today I can find some amusement in my entrée to the nation's capital. I still carry the reminders, however. The ailment turned out to be Crohn's Disease, which is chronic and lifelong – although treatable – and my life as a captive of the western medical world began.

Drugs are the weapons of choice here in the West. And hydrocortisone steroids, under the name of prednisone, are the recommended treatment for chronic inflammation of the large intestine, which is where my particular form of the disease unpacked its easy chair and ottoman.

Prednisone is a powerful drug. If you take enough, it can certainly wipe out your original symptoms. But take 60 mg. of it a day and it's like jump-starting your car by attaching your battery to a nuclear reactor.

The side effects are legion: insomnia, racing mind, crazy thoughts, excessive sweating, muscle pulls and tears, and developing "moon face" after several weeks of treatment. What's worse is when you taper off prednisone and finally get to a low dose. It caused such bad skin that I started referring to my face as David's Acne Ranch.

So after 11 years in the fun house of hydrocortisone, I turned my glance toward the East, looking for more gentle alternatives. And I think I may have found one in a culinary lifestyle called macrobiotics.

Simply stated, macrobiotics is the notion that eating in harmony with one's environment can create balance and restore health.

OK, stop giggling. I know it sounds wacky, like something a crazy Californian would do. But in all fairness, I actually am a Californian now and the weirdest thing is that it seems to work.

Shifting to a macrobiotic diet requires such a psychological shift it's not for the faint of heart. You eliminate most everything near and dear to the western epicure: no meats, no dairy products, no sugar, no alcohol, no tropical fruits, no tomatoes, no potatoes. No Strawberry Twizzlers.

And you replace all this with a way of eating centered on short-grained, organically grown brown rice. Other choices from nature's palette include millet, barley and quinoa – the power food of the Incas (who might still be around if it weren't for smallpox and that bastard Pizarro).

You supplement this basic fare with many of the fresh vegetables you hated as a child, assorted seaweeds and a litany of such exotic protein sources as turtle, adzuki and navy beans; red and green lentils; and tofu and tempeh.

The beans and lentils took some getting used to from a gastroenterological standpoint. To be delicate, let's just say there were a couple of weeks when you didn't want to do any arc welding around me.

A friend of mine lit a cigarette after we had dinner at his place one time and we're still looking for him. We found his watch and underwear on a fence outside, but that's been pretty much it.

As for the seaweed, I've eaten so much lately I'm afraid I'm going to wake up one morning with a blowhole on the top of my head.

If this isn't enough to frighten you off a macrobiotic diet, there is some genuine horror-show stuff in this new regimen. Take miso, for example.

Miso is a high-protein paste made from soybeans and a type of fungus, which is used primarily in soup stock. Although the soup can be delicious in Japanese restaurants, miso itself is one of the nastiest substances this side of Vegemite. It has a distinctive aroma that should be familiar to anyone who has ever cleaned up after a college keg party. The smell of miso is a dead nasal ringer for the odor of stale beer tastefully accentuated with floating cigarette butts.

I may roast in Zen Hell for this, but I'm taking a pass on the miso.

Strangely, my system seems to agree with this new routine, despite the inordinate amount of time required to procure and prepare meals and the general unavailability of quick cures for a growling tummy, especially when you're traveling.

Of course, I also have to suffer the constant suspicion of people who disdain anything outside the narrow bands of western convention. I've already had my share of comments from peckish hosts. One of them stared at me after I explained my dietary requirements and said, "Why don't you just go outside and graze on the lawn?"

I have a simple question for these people – and for anyone else who reacts to my choice of a macrobiotic lifestyle with intolerance: Are you going to eat the other half of your sandwich?

Note: *Conversations and activities with my children have been the source of several of these articles. In this one, my dear daughter Ellery really did burst into my bedroom (she and her twin brother Owen always "burst" into my bedroom) and she really did have a question. I tried my best to answer, but – as is often the case – something went awry.*

Nature's Power Bar

Last night, my high-school-aged daughter burst into my bedroom with a question.

"Fadré, what's placenta?" she asked.

She's been calling me Fadré so long that I don't even notice it anymore. It's her creative combination of Father plus Padre. God forbid that anyone in my family would use a common nickname, such as Dad. It reminds me of the acorn and the oak and everything that implies.

"Well, Sweetheart," I said, launching into a detailed answer, "it's an organ that connects a baby in the womb to the mother's uterus and assists with nutrient and oxygen intake as well as waste exchange. When you and your brother were born, you each had a separate placenta because you're fraternal twins."

And since no one in my family can answer a question without jumping into a story, I proceeded.

"After the two of you finished popping out of your Mom, the obstetrician led me around to the end of the delivery table and there was what looked like a blue children's wading pool on the floor. It had both placentas floating in it and she wanted to show me."

"Gross!"

"Yes, there was a bit of that," I said. "But it was fascinating, too."

She wrinkled her face and asked another question.

"Don't people eat placenta?"

"Hmm," I replied, stalling for time and trying to think through the possibilities. "I don't think so. Maybe in some very primitive and remote cultures they might eat the placenta, but I think it's rare. Some tribes even bury the placenta because they think of it as having been alive. Most hospitals incinerate them. But it's common for animals to eat the placenta, especially ungulates."

"What's an ungulate? That thing that hangs down in your throat and gets all swollen when you're sick?"

"That's your uvula, Honey. Ungulates are horses, deer, antelopes, zebras. Animals like those."

"Oh."

"Once I was at the San Diego Zoo early in the morning and some of the antelope had given birth the day before," I continued. "There were placentas all over the enclosure where the mothers had lain down to deliver their babies. You could tell the mothers had eaten some or all of the placentas.

"They're very rich in nutrients and nature doesn't like to waste valuable things like that. So the antelopes eat them. It helps the animals get their strength back quickly after birth so they can get away from predators as soon as they can."

"I thought I'd read that people eat it," she said.

"They eat placentas? No, that can't be right," said the all-knowing authority on everything in the world. You don't need Google with me around.

"Maybe the mother eats a lot of corn," she said.

"Eats corn? What does that have to do with a placenta?"

And then it hit me — a bit slow on the uptake, as always — and I shook my head.

"You don't mean placenta, do you? I think you're asking about polenta."

"Polenta, placenta, whatever," she said.

"It's a side dish or entrée made with boiled corn meal."

"Great, Fadré. Thanks!"

"And all that stuff I told you about ungulates and your mother, and you and your brother and the wading pool?"

"Yes?"

"Just forget it."

"You got it, Fadré!"

Maybe the next time she asks me something, I'll do a little probing before I show off with the wrong answer. It's also going to be a long, long time before I eat polenta again.

Note: *Satire reigns again in Tieline East. At the time of this column, Hewlett-Packard was undergoing the first job-reduction campaign since I became an employee in 1987. There was no way we representatives of the employee perspective could take this lying down, so I stood up for the trod-upon — at a safe distance from corporate headquarters.*

For a long time, some friends throughout the Eastern Sales Region kept asking me if I really did get rid of the cat. The answer: No, of course not. It was satire, my friends, simply satire. Published in spring 1991.

Of Mice and Mulch

We agonized over the decision, we really did. But the more we thought about it, the more we realized there were no better alternatives.

Our profitability had been eroding steadily over the past few years. Many of our processes had become cumbersome and inefficient. The shareholders were breathing down our necks, demanding a better return on their investments.

So we bit the bullet. Last month, we reorganized the Price family.

As with all good reorganizations, we started at the top. My wife and I established a chief executive office where we would share responsibility for all major decisions. Each of us considered this a promotion.

Then we established a Management Committee so our major plans could be reviewed before implementation. We figured this would eliminate a great deal of rework, such as the kind required when your spousal unit discovers you've had 10 cubic yards of shredded mulch delivered over night and there's a mountain of the stuff in the driveway behind her car, which she had actually planned to drive to work. And now she's wondering what in the world possessed her to marry a man with the IQ of sweater lint. That sort of thing.

Next, we streamlined the organization below us, dividing it into two specific product groups. Our three felines comprised the first, which needed a new name to reflect its new responsibilities: Mouse-Eating Organisms with Whiskers (MEOW).

Then there was the fish question. For years they were bundled into the same organization as the cats, severely curtailing their potential for growth. We needed to separate them into their own group, with a distinct marketing organization, so they could develop into a world-class operation. They're now part of our second unit: the Global League of Underwater Beings (GLUB).

With the new names came strict demands for increased productivity. The fish simply had to improve their ventral line. Otherwise, we'd have no choice but to redeploy them down the toilet bowl.

Flush from our success with streamlining the organization, we attacked the issue of headcount. Our employee base stood at 14: two top executives, three members of MEOW and nine employees in GLUB. Historically, our attrition rate has been low, except for the unfortunate incident when a member of a third-party cleaning crew left the entrance to GLUB open and several employees disappeared.

Since attrition wasn't the answer, we had no option but to take an excruciatingly difficult action. Last week, with a great deal of reluctance, we declared Ceci, our junior cat, as "excess."

And I want to say for the record that her habit of attacking my bare ankles with her claws first thing in the morning as if she were Edward Scissorhands with an attitude had nothing to do with it. Or the way she'd leap onto my face at four in the morning to alert the executive staff that her food supply had diminished. These eccentricities weren't the primary reason. It was strictly a business decision.

Thank goodness everything turned out for the best. Ceci decided to move on to a neighboring company rather than pursue opportunities elsewhere in our town. She seems quite happy when I see her. And in some ways, she's better off than we are.

You see, Ceci was the best mouser in our MEOW organization despite her tender years. Since she's gone, a new family of the little beasts is proliferating in our woodpile, undoubtedly plotting an all-out attack on our headquarters.

Thanks to my success with the mulch project, the Management Committee has placed me in charge of the Mouse Removal Task Force. Although rodent removal is not one of my core capabilities, we all need to assume additional responsibilities in these lean times and do the best we can.

In fact, I should get going. The mouse situation is escalating. And there's all that mulch to move.

I do understand and appreciate the need for these tough decisions, by the way. But there are still times when I really miss our little Ceci.

It was nothing personal, of course. Just business in America in the 1990s. Just business in America.

Note: *Although I heartily agree that one shouldn't show favorites among children, I do have a special affection for this story. I had moved to a Washington, D.C.-area apartment in summer 1980 and became fiercely sick with full-blown Crohn's Disease that October – two weeks before qualifying for health insurance.*

So I'm in a new city with a new job, I'm a couple of thousand dollars in debt and my girlfriend had just left me to go back to the man she was going to marry in the first place (long story). My body fell apart in response to all this stress and my immune system revolted.

Meanwhile, I always had this idea about how to save oneself if an elevator dropped and turned it into this story in summer 1981. My dear friend at the time, Bernie Keating, loved it and decided to illustrate it. He did a marvelous job and he presented the drawings to me as a gift sometime later, after I got married and we had a falling out.

Unfortunately, one of his illustrations disappeared during my several moves and I have no idea what happened either it or to Bernie. I've looked him up online on numerous occasions, but haven't been able to find him. Bernie?

Simon and the Elevator

I always take the stairs. Oh, there was a time I used to take elevators like everybody else. I would suffer through a pang of claustrophobia or xenophobia or any of my other phobias just to make the trip from the ground to a floor high up in the air.

But that was before I knew Simon.

Poor Simon was terrified of riding in an elevator. His anxiety went far beyond the garden-variety psychological ailments. Simon had a deathly fear that once he was suspended thirty floors up in an elevator shaft, the cables would snap, sending him screaming to a blind date with gravity.

Goodness knows, people tried to talk him out of it. Simon visited with counselors, psychiatrists, his local clergyman. He even met with engineers from elevator manufacturing firms who painstakingly assured him that the chances of such an occurrence were less than that of being eaten by a great white shark while getting hit by lightning.

He even wrote to Abby, who was sympathetic, but the fear persisted.

Only once in his life had Simon actually traveled in an elevator. As a child, his mother had taken him along on a luncheon excursion with her lady friends. On a lark, they gathered to dine at an exclusive bistro perched atop the tallest building in their medium-sized metropolis. The restaurant, called the Heavenly Flame, rested on the 27th floor like a birthday cake on a telephone pole. It was known for its scampi.

Simon's mother had been unable to find a babysitter. Instead of missing the affair, she bundled up her son on that chilly fall day and brought him along. Simon, at four years of age, clutched at his mother's dress when the party entered the elevator, oblivious to the treat everyone believed he was about to have.

The machine they stepped into was a local landmark. It glided up a glass and steel shaft on the outside edge of the building so tourists and locals alike could be enthralled by an unencumbered panorama as they swept upwards. It was quite a view. Some even say that the experience of rising to the highest vantage point in the city as if you were snugly nestled in Cinderella's glass slipper is better than the food.

The doors shut behind the happy clutch of women. The motors whirred and the elevator began its ascent. At the first movement, Simon stirred, wide-eyed, and tightened the grip on his mother's garment.

After only a few floors, Simon began making a high-pitched whining noise that matched the vibrations of the machine. With every increase in elevation, his distress mounted, displayed in the increasingly horrible sounds his shrill little voice was making.

By the time they hit the 15th floor, Simon was shrieking and holding on to his mother's dress so tightly that the eyehook guarding her lingerie from a public viewing popped from its threads and hit little Simon in the cheek.

Now he had a real reason to scream and scream he did. Whatever innate fears he held deep inside had been confirmed by this nudge from reality and his tantrum exploded. Simon screamed bloody murder, rolling around on the floor of the elevator and putting his tiny hands to his face to shield himself the best he could.

His mother tried to comfort him, but Simon fought with the strength of a bobcat in a trainer's noose. He refused to be consoled, even as the elevator spat its ruffled contents onto the 27th floor.

As the doors opened, Simon pried himself away from his mother's grip and crawled lickety-split to the nearest point of firm anchor, which happened to be the leg of the maître d'. He would not budge until his internal systems righted themselves several embarrassing minutes later.

When Simon's calm demeanor had been restored, apologies were exchanged and the ladies proceeded with lunch. Most ordered the Heavenly Flame's famous scampi and avocado salad with the house balsamic vinaigrette dressing.

When the gathering ended, the other ladies went down in the elevator on the insistence of Simon's mother. To her credit, the valiant woman accepted her fate gracefully and trundled her son down 27 flights of stairs.

Since that day, Simon avoided all elevators. Whenever business or pleasure required a physical ascent – no matter how high – Simon took the stairs with a quiet grace. If a companion complained, he would graciously escort her to the elevator door in the manner of a gentleman and insist he would meet her on the desired floor in just a few minutes.

The process worked well. Simon's quiet charm assured his companions that his peculiarity was not the rambling of a lunatic but simply a neurosis he had found a way to combat.

Fortunately for Simon, his town was relatively small. Life did not depend on the constant alteration of one's elevation to maintain sufficient business and social contacts. However, a few years later, Simon received the job opportunity of a lifetime.

A recruiter contacted him, Simon interviewed over the phone with several people and he was offered a terrific job in New York City. This new position would afford him a far more upscale lifestyle than he presently enjoyed, with a chance for a professionally and socially invigorating existence. In so many ways, it would have been foolish for Simon to decline the offer.

Except for one modest problem: the new job was in Manhattan and his office would be on the 47th floor. Now, Simon had the thighs and calves of a sprinter after all his years of walking up and down stairs. But New York offered a special challenge with all those massive skyscrapers.

He pondered the predicament. Simon had always desired such an opportunity. If it weren't for his terrible fear of elevators, he would have tried to get a job in New York years ago. After careful deliberation, Simon, in his wonderfully pragmatic way, decided that somehow he could do it. He accepted the offer.

Simon was not the type of man who kept his neurosis so tightly bottled up that the mere site of an elevator would send him into uncontrollable tremors. Quite the contrary – Simon was an engineer, and he examined the problem from innumerable angles, secretly hoping to find a solution. One day, with an epiphany so great it should be housed in the Smithsonian Institution, the answered appeared.

Physics, Simon's brain whispered one evening under the satin sheet of darkness and several ounces of 12-year-old bourbon. Of course, thought Simon, physics!

His mind made rapid progress after being roused by the hurricane winds of inspiration. Within days, Simon had a rough draft of a remarkable mathematic formula that seemed to render moot the only flaw in his personality. This arithmetic amulet turned the idea on its head – certainly an elevator cable can snap at an inopportune moment, leading to a terrible and fatal crash for the people trapped inside. But is it not possible to survive the crash? Simon's theory screamed, "Yes!"

With the quantum leaping of mathematic gazelles, Simon perfected a formula based on the weights of the elevators in the buildings he would frequent, incorporating the continuing variants of passenger weights and the friction coefficients for the materials on the inside of the elevator shafts. These elements could be quantified, he reasoned, so he could compute the rate of descent during a prospective disaster with the immutable laws of physics.

Simon inhaled information on the constant pull of gravity. With the aid of calculus and an expensive bathroom scale, he scampered down the path to freedom from his fear.

The answer had been so simple that Simon laughed whenever he thought about the solution. It went like this: If an elevator cable snaps in mid-air and the contents begin hurtling toward a rude reversal of velocity at the basement floor, the moment of impact can be calculated.

And here's where Simon's plan lifted itself to the lofty pinnacle of simple genius. If an occupant in the elevator knows the moment of impact, a split second before the crash he can merely jump straight up in the air so he is suspended when the impact occurs. This way, his own upward velocity will counteract that of the plunge and he will drop safely to the ground inside the smashed elevator with minor bruises at the worst.

Though certainly no trained physicist, it seemed logical enough to Simon. So he went to work putting his plan into action.

Simon conferred with the engineers who designed the elevator apparatus at each of the buildings he would most likely frequent. During these sessions, he picked their minds and blueprints for details as to construction, distances and the materials used. He calculated the rate of falling for each individual elevator and the distance from every conceivable spot in the shaft to the basement floor below.

After weeks of extensive research and number-crunching, Simon gleefully anticipated a trial run. It was balmy in New York on that memorable fall day. Simon awoke early in the second-floor hotel room he had rented. He showered, had a light breakfast, dressed and headed for the skyscraper where his new office would be. He had chosen a Sunday so he could launch his experiment unencumbered by other passengers.

By now, Simon was so thoroughly versed in the nuances of each elevator that they were like old friends to him. For his trial run, he chose elevator three, which he had nicknamed Dulcinea. Armed with his ultra-sensitive bathroom scale, a Hewlett-Packard scientific calculator, an expensive and accurate stopwatch, a yellow legal pad and a matching No. 2 pencil, Simon was ready.

He weighed himself outside the elevator doors, wrote down the figure on his pad and pressed the button marked "Up." There was a moment's hesitation, a brief vibration and a rattle before the silver doors opened. Simon took a long, deep breath and walked in.

When the doors closed, Simon pushed the "Stop" button on the inside panel and made some rapid calculations, scribbling them onto his pad. When he finished, he raised the stopwatch, pushed the button for the second floor and watched as the doors closed. At the first sign of upward movement, Simon plunged his thumb onto the stopwatch.

The elevator ascended smoothly, without a hint of trouble. Then it stopped, almost imperceptibly, at the next floor. The "2" lit up above the doors with an amber glow, not unlike the sun rising to kiss the eastern sky. The silver doors slid open. Simon stepped off.

He stood for a few moments, unable to discern any specific sensation as the impact of his victory swirled inside. The corners of his mouth gave way first, spreading into a grin.

"I did it!" Simon shouted, prancing down the second-floor corridor and dancing with the potted fig trees.

He spent the rest of the day giddily experimenting with his scheme. He rode from floor to floor, rapidly calculating, preparing for the worst at all times. At the end of the day, nearly exhausted from the effort, Simon made the grand voyage – 84 floors up and down – which was a pilgrimage on par with a jostling mare's ride to Canterbury. It was exhilarating, even fun, and Simon felt cleansed.

For the next several weeks, he fine-tuned the plan and prepared for dealing with any variations in his formulas. Of prime importance during this phase was Simon's natural gift of charm, which was sorely needed during rush hour in New York. Simon still required complete and accurate information on all fellow passengers, which meant weighing everyone before they got on and computing the weights of anyone entering or leaving on any subsequent floors. But Simon's victory over his only fear gave him such an aura of fulfillment that most everyone was willing to deal with his eccentricity and wait. If someone spat out that slang term for intercourse that can be angrily used in gerund form to modify assorted nouns such as "idiot," "dirtball" and "scum bucket," Simon simply apologized and waited for the next elevator.

His fear under control, Simon developed his business skills and personal contacts. He soon blossomed in Gotham town. He lived well, had the respect of his colleagues and enjoyed life to the utmost in the cultural center of the western world.

Still, somewhere far down a corridor in his mind, back in the eerie crevasses of dank, rarely traveled pathways – far from the bustle of daily nervous-system activity – a child whimpered, clutching the leg of a stranger in a rented tuxedo.

Twelve years passed since Simon emerged victorious from his first New York City elevator ride. He celebrated by attending a dinner party with some influential friends on a Saturday night. The menu featured filet mignon and scallops as the main course, with fine wines poured liberally throughout the evening.

Simon had not taken even a sip of alcohol in almost five years, deciding long ago that he was better off without it. He declined the first pouring of Pinot Noir as he always did, but the attractive European woman with the chestnut hair and the push-up brassiere next to him smiled and offered him a sip from her glass. He sniffed that magic elixir and remembered how much he missed the ambiance and the ritual of drinking wine.

"Oh, what harm will it do?" Simon thought to himself. "I can control it now. It's just wine."

He motioned for the waiter to bring over the bottle and pour him a glass. Simon swirled the blood-red liquid and watched the viscous legs ease down the sides. He put the glass to his lips and let the first sip caress his tongue. Then he swallowed, feeling the alcohol slide down his throat and into his stomach, where it passed into his bloodstream and raced to his brain.

Hours later, he left the party alone and decided on a whim to drop by his office and pick up some papers so he could prepare for the coming week.

With the lobby of his building deserted, Simon let himself in with his key card. Just as the door was shutting behind him, an old woman wearing an oversized coat as a buffer against the evening's chill scuttled in behind him. Simon was a bit surprised by her appearance, but, being an amiable sort, he said hello and tried to strike up a brief conversation.

The woman explained that she had left some things behind when she went home earlier. She had returned, hoping the building would still be unlocked.

They chatted quietly about the weather and other little niceties, wandering over to where Dulcinea, the third elevator, awaited them. The old woman pressed the "Up" button and

Simon launched into his explanation of how he would need to know her weight if they intended to travel together.

The woman gave him a quizzical look and Simon was about to suggest they go their separate ways when she blurted out, "97!"

Simon asked if she would mind verifying that figure with his own scale. He pulled the instrument from his briefcase.

"It's 97 exactly," she said, "clothes included. And my bag here weighs 6.3 pounds." She indicated the small valise she carried.

The elevator had arrived by now and the doors opened lazily, inviting them inside. Simon was politely turning to find another elevator when the old woman cocked her head and addressed him.

"How about you?"

"I beg your pardon?" Simon asked.

"How much do you weight, sport?" the old woman asked. "I gotta know."

With that, the old woman pulled a worn bathroom scale from her bag and set it on the floor.

"Well, um, I, uh, weigh 172," Simon said, intrigued by this development.

"The briefcase?" asked the old woman, pointing at the shiny black leather valise.

"8.5," he answered.

"Okay," she said, retrieving the scale. "That sounds right. Let's go."

Simon hesitated for an instant, but was reasonably sure the woman was telling the truth. After all, wasn't he an expert on size and weight? He had pretty much seen it all in his 12 years of calculating. Simon thought hard. The glasses of wine he had with dinner told him everything was OK. The child inside his head rolled over onto his side. He slumbered.

Simon sighed and followed the old woman into the elevator. She turned her back to him in the corner, immediately engrossed in some rapid writing. Simon had no time to question her because he had to plot the variations on his formula.

When he finished calculating, he pressed "47" on the elevator's console; the woman must have pressed "51" because the light behind the number glowed. The doors slid closed.

The elevator began its quiet climb upwards in the same way it always had. It was the smoothest of all the elevators in the building and had become Simon's favorite. Dulcinea had never so much as rumbled in his 12 years of travel.

Simon finished his variations quickly and had his pre-designed chart close at hand. The old woman kept her back to him in the corner of the elevator and mumbled softly to herself.

The elevator continued upward, the lights blinking softly in sequence: 21, 22, 23. The progression was as unbending as always.

But as the elevator passed the 28th floor, the light didn't go on.

That's odd, thought Simon. Usually maintenance keeps a close eye on such things.

Twenty-nine asserted itself as normal, so Simon thought little of the custodial shortcomings. They'll fix it Monday morning, he reasoned.

As they passed 34, a peculiar hum seemed to filter through the walls of the elevator. It was hard to notice at first, but by the time "35" winked at Simon and the old woman, a definitive whine pierced the quiet – like the vibrations of a tightly strung guy wire that's been struck with a pipe wrench.

The old woman spun around.

"You hear something, sport?" she asked.

"I'm not quite certain," Simon replied.

"Hit 37, quick," she squawked, pulling a pad of paper from her worn bag, along with something that glimmered.

Simon reached for the console, but the elevator lurched to a halt, throwing them both to the floor. And instead of holding solid as most elevators do when they're stuck between floors, Dulcinea swayed measurably from side to side.

Both passengers scrambled to their feet and the old woman scurried to the corner away from Simon.

"Here we go, kiddo," she said, with a peculiar tone of anticipation.

Simon was not paying any attention to her. He was rifling through his charts, pinpointing the distance figures from every conceivable portion of the shaft between the 36th and 37th floors. In one hand he had his charts; the other held his prized stopwatch, primed to measure any possible descent.

The elevator rocked once to the right, crashing Simon into the wall and sending the old woman to her knees.

"It's all right," she said, with an odd calm. "It's all right."

Simon could not concern himself with answering. The humming had increased to an irritating decibel level and the elevator shifted hard to the left. Simon fell to the floor as the sound of steel shattering in a frozen echo chamber pierced the elevator walls. Dulcinea lurched to the right and the sound of tearing metal shrieked through the machine. There was a moment of eerie quiet. Then the vessel dropped.

Simon hit his stopwatch. He kept his wits about him as the elevator plunged into the void. The moment the sweep hits .124, I jump, he thought. It's been planned. Everything's fine. It will work perfectly. There's no need to panic. 1...2...4.

The numbers on the stopwatch sprinted in their tight circle – the only focal point in a reeling world, moving relentlessly amid the chaos. We're almost there, Simon thought, laughing with the giddiness of speed and tension. We're almost there. Be ready. OK. Be set. OK. Here we go. Right...

Before he jumped, Simon noticed a faint apparition in the corner of his eye, sailing slightly upward. He sensed the movement more than seeing it, but – whatever it was – it distracted him just enough that his feet never left the elevator floor as the cube of metal and glass slammed into the hard concrete of the bottom of the shaft. He never jumped.

Twelve years of preparing for this very moment. Twelve years of constant vigilance, always certain he would survive, always keeping consummate faith in his calculations. But he never jumped.

Simon managed to struggle up onto one mangled elbow with his last bit of strength. He surveyed the wreckage. The pain overwhelmed his nervous system, virtually canceling itself out and allowing his brain one final bout with reason.

He looked up through the dust and twisted metal. To his utter amazement, he saw the old woman, rising to her feet and dusting herself off. She had an odd gleam in her peculiar eyes and was clutching the baggy coat at her chest.

Simon stared at her, telegraphing the confusion in his faltering brain. A question formed at his lips, but as he struggled to spit the words from his mouth, the old woman's chest heaved.

She's hurt as badly as I am, Simon thought. He tried to reach out to her, to comfort her in their final moments. But his hand fell short as his strength seeped into the air. Her chest pulsed in response to his gesture. Simon felt himself lapsing into unconsciousness, mesmerized by the old woman's chest.

It heaved again and again, each spasm swelling with such violence that Simon thought her organs would surely burst through the fabric. He began to ease his eyes away from that impending sight when, with a final thrust, a large gray-and-black-striped face poked its way to freedom between the buttons of her coat and shook itself.

The old woman smiled, looking down at Simon.

"The cat weighs 10," she said.

So I always take the stairs.

Note: *If you're feeling stressed trying to get through our busy, busy modern lives, you may relate to this article. It was published as part of the Apparently So columns at Hewlett-Packard in 2000. I revised it, making the day even more stressful, in 2009.*

Stressed for Success

It's been happening every night for a week now. After I change out of my T-shirt and jeans, brush my teeth and say my prayers, I climb into bed and place my weary head on my pillow.

As I lay there, I replay the day's craziness in my mind: a work pace that would kill a jackrabbit, the constant deadline pressure from working on my experiments, the needs of my children, and all those tasks and chores I didn't have time to do.

I toss and turn for what seems like hours until the Trazodone kicks in and I finally slip into the arms of Morpheus. Then, every night, as regular as a German nutritionist, the dream starts.

I'm sitting in an enormous pipe that stretches as far as you can see in either direction. It's quiet in there, except for an occasional drip that echoes through the dank metal tube.

My head starts nodding and I'm about to fall asleep in my dream when a voice that sounds like Hannah Montana on helium screams, "Howdy, y'all!" and breaks into maniacal laughter.

In the distance, I hear a rumbling sound that's getting louder and louder. I look up and see the cause of the commotion: A huge wave of water, filled with peculiar objects, is raging down the pipe and heading straight for me.

As the wave rumbles closer, I spy Kim Kardashian, floating on breasts the size of ice cream trucks, as if they were gigantic water wings. Riding on Kim's back is celebrity fossil Joan Rivers, who's wrapped in a red carpet. She's tugging at Kim's hair and screaming, "What are you doing? I said I need a lift! I need a lift!"

They rush away and a half-dozen members of a Welsh rugby team swirl by, jogging in place and chanting a Dylan Thomas poem about canaries. They're on the roof of an enormous black SUV with Tony Soprano at the wheel. He's shaving his heavy beard with an old-fashioned straight razor that's dripping with blood as he reads the Wall Street Journal and weaves through rush-hour traffic.

Up pops the woman who emcees the pledge drive for my local public broadcasting station. She's standing on a raft of unsolicited direct mail, screaming that I'll never see the final episode of "The Mating Dance of the Australian Cheek Warbler," until I send her $10,000.

Then the river hits me with the force of a tornado in a telephone booth and I'm swept underwater, gasping for air.

I usually wake up about then, thank goodness. I shake the madness out of my head, pry the cats off my face and roll out of bed – primed for another day on the Tilt-a-Whirl of life in the 21st Century.

Does your life seem like it's raging out of control? Are you constantly stretched in multiple ways as if each of your limbs is attached to a team of plow horses who were just shot in their muscular bums with a dart gun and who are now angrily running off in four different directions?

Whether it's the competing demands of work or your children or your parents or your friends or volunteer activities or exercising or all of them together? Fixing breakfast, fixing lunch, getting the kids out the door, but your son forgot to get your signature on his PE homework so you have to run back inside for a pen. You sign the form, pile into the car, drop them at school and make an illegal U-turn. Somebody honks and you flash them the bird as you drive off to work where you can't get anything completed because no one cares about your deadlines and everything's a crisis and your boss is a micro-managing lunatic when he isn't hitting on you.

During your 30 minutes for lunch, you try to run as many as you can of the two dozen errands you couldn't get to during the weekend with all the play dates and soccer games and photo days and taking everyone for a hike and visiting your mother and making dinner for your friends because it's your turn and grocery shopping at the three different stores it takes to find all the things you and the kids like. And the children need baseball cleats and ballet shoes and underwear and the dog is out of kibble and your daughter's hamster has to have that special kind of food that it likes, oh, and those little chew toys, too?

Of course, everyone else is out running their two dozen errands and traffic is worse than rush hour. You finally find a parking space a half mile from the store's entrance, dash inside, find what you need and the man at the front of the line finds out that the magnum-size bottle of Grey Goose vodka isn't the one on sale – it requires a mail-in rebate form – so he asks for the form and the clerk, who could not care less because who wants a job like this anyway?, slowly tries to find it in the stack of papers next to the register.

He finally decides to forget it and walks away but you have to get back for the 1:00 meeting and the lady in front of you decides she wants stamps, but then doesn't have enough money for them anyway after a careful search of every last crumbling piece of lint in her ancient purse. They finally check you out, you run to your car, back out and drive to the office, and you're just about to make the meeting except your ex-husband calls on the way and he can't remember if he's supposed to take the deduction for Christopher on his taxes or little Isabella because he can't find the Marital Separation Agreement. He needs the information right now because he's meeting with his accountant at 1:00 and, sorry, he could have called you a week ago, but he forgot.

And your call-waiting bleeps and you recognize the number so you put your ex on hold and it's your dad's nursing home saying they can't get him off the roof again and is it OK to tranquilize him this time?

When you finally do manage to get home for the day, feed the kids, water the plants, tend to the animals, pay the bills, clean the kitchen and finally have a moment for yourself, you're too tired to do anything but have a glass of wine. And as you start to relax, your neighbor's kid – the renters – starts practicing with his garage band and the drums thud and rattle and crash as the electric guitar pierces the air like a wolverine with its tail caught in the disposer and you want to call the police but you hate conflict and you have to live with these people so you take two Ambien and another glass of wine and you go to bed and you toss and turn yourself to sleep, and you keep having these strange dreams?

Does any of this sound familiar? If so, my friend, you may be suffering from what we in medicine call the silent killer: Stress.

In strict scientific terms, stress results from having dozens of things to do and only the mental, physical, emotional and spiritual bandwidth to handle somewhere around nine of them. Stress can cause heart palpitations, increased blood pressure, gastric upset, shortness of breath and – according to a groundbreaking study at the Cambridge Medical University – an uncontrollable urge to stand up on your couch or desk and sing songs from "My Fair Lady."

We're seeing this tragic sight more and more often in these tumultuous times of ours. Out of nowhere, someone will suddenly hop onto his desk and sing:

> "I have often walked
> down this street before
> but the pavement always stayed
> beneath my feet before..."

Although modern medicine has been doing its best to treat the symptoms of stress-related illnesses (SRIs), the leading medical associations are baffled as to a cure. They have recommended everything from acupuncture and Zen meditation to individual therapy and neural stimulation, but you've come to me because of my innovative, even revolutionary, approach.

Last year, I was awarded a federal grant of almost five figures to study my radical proposal for curing SRIs. While most doctors recommend developing coping skills or taking medication to cope with the escalating demands of our modern world, I believe they're concentrating on the wrong end of the problem. My contrarian hypothesis is that — instead of treating the symptoms — we should be working to increase a human being's capacity (in layman's language) "to do stuff."

You may recall an experiment they forced us to perform in high-school chemistry. We stirred a granular solid (sugar) into a stable liquid (iced tea) until a small mound of solid (gunk) formed at the bottom of the beaker. Great, we thought. Time for lunch.

But there was more. The liquid had reached what we professional scientists refer to as "the saturation point." You could stir that beaker like a monkey on meth, but it would not dissolve one more crystal of sugar.

However, as our teacher explained, as the temperature of a solution is raised, its capacity to dissolve a solid increases. Aha! So we fired up our Bunsen burners, applied them to the bottom of the beakers and, Voila! We produced the sweetest iced tea outside of Athens, Georgia, itself.

Using the same logic employed at the highest levels of government, if something works this well with iced tea, why not try it with humans?

Moments ago, I lit a Bunsen burner and placed it under my chair. Already I'm starting to type at least 40 percent faster. I've created three new word-processing files and am writing and editing multiple medical journal articles on my discovery, all at the same time. I'm also entering the data I'm collecting into two different spreadsheets while creating Power Point slides for the presentation I plan to give at a medical conference next month.

I just called my publicist, too, and we're discussing the media strategy for the book I'm writing. I'm working beautifully – thinking, writing, planning, talking – going like gangbusters. I'm working faster and faster, churning out the production of a dozen communication workers – although I am getting a little hotter now and sweat seems to be dripping down my face and my chair is smoking and...

Hey! What's this? Some force seems to have taken control of my legs. I don't know why, but I'm rising to my feet. I'm, I'm climbing onto my desk. Hey! What is this? Why am I clearing my throat? Why am I about to...

"I'm getting married in the morning
Spruced up and looking in my prime!"

Rats. It's "My Fair Lady" again. Another great idea, up in smoke.

Note: *When Lew Platt decided to retire as chief executive officer of HP, I stepped forward – fool's hat jingling – and offered my help for selecting an appropriate successor. Based on my experience writing internal messages for Lew (something I was slated to do for the next CEO, too), who better than I to lay out what traits are required to adequately perform the duties of the company leader?*

For the record, I also accurately predicted that the next CEO would be a woman. This appeared in Apparently So in late May 1999.

Summer of 42 Long

I know this about myself: The less somebody asks for my help, the more inclined I am to give it. As we're well aware, the once and future Hewlett-Packard needs a new chief executive officer. And who's more qualified than we are to help the matchmakers find us a perfect match?

HP is currently working with a fancy-schmancy search team that's burning their billable hours and shaking the high-tech trees for possible candidates. I fully believe a homegrown effort to crown the people's choice is a much better idea, one that would save us trash bags full of dollars and yen. So let's do it.

As background, I've already suggested a simple, cost-effective solution to my good friend and current CEO Lew Platt (Oh, did I drop a name there?).

Truth be known, I've had the pleasure of working with our fearless leader on a regular basis over the past two years or so.

The other day, I asked him how the CEO search was going. His facial response reminded me yet again that I never want to sit across from him at a poker table.

Emboldened by my fourth cup of tea, I rushed in, the bells jingling on my fool's cap.

"I know how to save the company a lot of money on this," I said.

"How?" asked Lew.

"Make *me* the CEO," I replied. "By the time they figure out just how incompetent I am, I will have stashed away enough money to retire on."

He didn't even laugh.

"I've heard worse ideas," he said.

Since there's no way we can leave our beloved Lew Platt with worse ideas, we're off (but only slightly) on an unofficial campaign to name the next HP CEO.

First, we need to establish some criteria for what we need in a candidate. Based on my career-long observations of senior executives, I already have a brief list of absolute requirements for the position. To wit:

A bladder of steel. Senior executives spend most of their days in gluteal-numbing meetings, starting at the crack of dawn, so to speak, and ending with the cracking of their joints as they try to stand 16 hours later. What do they do during these marathon meetings? Well, lots of stuff – most of it accompanied by massive amounts of coffee drinking. And you can't just pop in and out of those meetings. Wander away for a quick bio break and somebody might take $10 million out of your budget. So a jumbo-sized, tightly disciplined, Bota bag of a bladder is the number-one requirement.

Little need for sleep. Let's face it, a CEO has to work those 16-hour days, go home, feed the dog, eat dinner, watch the ESPN sports highlights, wade through e-mail and the reading pile, and then hang upside down in the closet like Dracula to sleep for a couple of hours. Then they wake up pressed, refreshed, ready to do it again — six or seven days a week.

Unaffected by world travel. I once worked for an HP vice president who ran a worldwide manufacturing organization. He was always jetting off to Boeblingen, Germany; or Singapore or Tokyo. He'd arrive, solve a few problems, hold some meetings, kick some butts, make a few coffee-talk speeches, hold informal sessions with small groups of employees and check his voicemail. Then he'd turn around, fly back, get home late at night and still arrive at his desk, bright-eyed and alert, at 7:00 a.m. the next morning.

During that period of my HP life, I was commuting 2,419 frequent-flier miles between Rockville, Maryland, and Cupertino, California, at least twice a month. I'd leave early in the morning, fly for five hours, rent a car, zip down Highway 280 from the San Francisco airport to Cupertino, arrive at a meeting around noon (thanks to the time change) and fall asleep face down in the pizza by 3:00 p.m.

Wear a jacket that's at least a 42 Long. This is a pet theory of mine. Forget its sexist bias for a moment — I might surprise you on that count in a minute. But for many years, any male I've ever met who was either an executive or hot on the executive career path, had a jacket size of at least 42 Long, which means they had to be at least six feet tall with a 42-inch chest. (That's 183 and 107 cm., respectively, for my metric-minded friends.)

Since I come from a long line of short Welsh coal miners (the shorter they are, the more you can stuff into a coal mine), I've always found this both fascinating and discriminatory. But with the exception of your occasional Bill Gates, for a male executive candidate, it's 42 Long or Bust.

For the curious among us, Lew is a 44 Long – making him eminently qualified for CEO-dom. Keep in mind that this requirement is waived for a female candidate, unless you want to be led by Xena: Warrior Princess.

World-class information storage capacity. A CEO needs to have a near-photographic memory and an astounding ability to quickly access a diverse and voluminous amount of information – whether it's the name of someone's spouse that he or she met once five years ago or the return-on-asset performance of the most obscure division in the company.

I have to make a list so I can remember the three things I need at the hardware store. Then I have to go back at least once because I forgot to write down one of them.

That's it – my informal list of the five must-haves for the new CEO. And here's one more thought. Years ago, I read an article on the demographics and personal characteristics of the CEOs of the top *Fortune* 100 Companies. At the time it was published, every last one of them was a male. And here's the kicker: According to the article, not one of them owned a cat. "Too independent," was the typical reason stated.

Things have changed somewhat since that article appeared. There are more women CEOs these days, even in the Y-chromosome-drenched high-tech industry. But it wouldn't surprise me if the demographics haven't changed all that much.

So here's my final, very personal criterion for Hewlett-Packard's new CEO: I'd like to see a woman get the job. Of course, she has to be qualified, charismatic, brilliant and a fan of smart-aleck columnists, too. But I'd like to see it happen.

I don't have any particular reason for this or any facts to back me up – as usual. It's just a gut feeling. Call it intuition if you want.

You know what else? I'd also like her to have a cat.

Duly Noted: *In July 1999, Carly Fiorina was named CEO of Hewlett-Packard Company. Except for the 42 Long requirement (which was automatically waived for female candidates anyway), she met all the criteria above except for one slight disappointment. Ms. Fiorina describes herself as "an animal nut" and has owned several Yorkshire terriers, which – in the eyes of many – could actually qualify as cats.*

Note: *My lifetime appreciation for fireworks spawned this column and my credentials include running a fireworks stand in Littleton, Colorado, at the age of 16 with my next-door neighbor, Diane Dittemore, having nightly fire-cracker wars with neighborhood friends, and purchasing fireworks legally in North Carolina and setting them off illegally on the Outer Banks with my children and other family members.*

While the Chinese may be troublesome from a governmental standpoint, they sure make great fireworks, especially the double mortars that explode into gorgeous bursts of sound and colors. Somehow my mind turned this into an article for Apparently So, published in December 1998.

Happy Flower

I hate clichés especially when I'm in a bad, curmudgeonly mood instead of my more typical happy self. I've had enough of Web and television marketing people especially and all the other writers who say they're going to "turn a dream into reality." And if I ever hear someone say something "isn't exactly rocket science," I'm going to mail them a list of a dozen better ways to make their point, along with a crate of ravenous female brown recluse spiders, said to be the most poisonous in the world.

There are plenty more examples. Whenever someone dismisses a problem by saying "Well, it isn't exactly brain surgery," I feel my frontal lobe melt into warm cherry Jell-O and pour out my ears.

Or when you ask a simple question and the person responds, "If I tell you, I'll have to kill you," then laughs out loud. Cheese Whiz.

There are more than 400,000 words in the English language. According to my advanced mathematics, this means there are at least a dozen different ways to say all these hoary clichés and, yes, I know this is the curmudgeonly side of me speaking and I apologize for slipping into it.

But the absolute worst for me are the constant jokes about the fear and loathing inspired by this combination of words: root canal. "Oh, I'd rather have a *root canal*, than do such-and-such," people say. "Well, at least it's better than having a *root canal*." And everyone in the studio audience laughs.

Now, I know the idea of a root canal conjures frightening images of backhoes, front-loaders, dynamite, picks, shovels and mules – all carving their initials on the sensitive tissues of the inside of your mouth. But this is where marketing can actually do us some good for a change.

Why don't we invent a less horrifying name for this endodontic procedure – one that eliminates, or at least softens, the dread of anticipation?

The Chinese have the right idea, at least when it comes to naming fireworks. They take what is essentially the violent explosion of combustible chemical compounds and bestow whimsical names upon them.

My kids and I used to go to the beach at the Outer Banks of North Carolina every year for summer vacation and we always stopped at this certain store that sells wonderful illegal fireworks from the back room. In the front of the store, they also have rows and rows of legal things, such as colorfully packaged fountains from China, each bearing names like "Happy Flower," "Flowing Rainbow" or "Three Chrysanthemums."

Since perception is everything in our world – which explains some of the contestants' success on *American Idol* – a positive mental framework can achieve wonders and pull me right out of this cantankerous state of mind.

I suggest you give this a try. Whenever you need to do anything particularly unpleasant – like going on hold for computer or benefits support, having a one-on-one review with your boss, breaking up with a boyfriend or girlfriend, working your way through a voice-recognition answering system when you have a cold, or even actually *having* a root canal – give the task a whimsical name. If you can't think of anything on your own, feel free to use "Uncle Harry", "Barefoot Bob" or even "Happy Flower" itself.

I'll show you how it works. My former wife and I used to have periodic "business meetings," where we would discuss all the flotsam that had accumulated in our little lagoon during the past few weeks. By the time we'd gotten our children to bed and the daily chores out of the way, we were tired, crabby and in no mood for the delicate negotiating skills required in any joint marital activity. The mere phrase "business meeting," made us as snarly as a pair of wolverines with hangnails.

So I mentioned the Chinese fireworks phenomenon and we decided to start calling our meetings "Happy Flower" instead. It worked fabulously. We would put "Happy Flower" on our calendars and announce it at the beginning of our meetings. The simple silliness of the name took the edge off and let us get down to business with a mutually better attitude.

So try it. I mean, really. Which would you rather have? A root canal? Or a "Happy Flower"? Do you want to break up with your boyfriend? Or have a "Flowing Rainbow" instead?

And the final word on root canals? I've had four of them in my life so I'm completely familiar with the procedure. With a good endodontist, properly applied Novocain and some simple meditation techniques, guess what? They're not that big of a deal. They're not exactly rocket science.

Oh, crud. That just slipped out. I'd better...

Ow! Hey! Get those spiders off me!

Note: Here's a fun one from Apparently So that got me into a boiling cauldron of trouble. An important New Company executive didn't want me to get the Hewlett-Packard employees involved in naming the new test-and-measurement company that was splitting off from HP. When he saw the column below, his cerebral cortex blew hotter than grits on a southern grill.

My manager, mentor and dear friend Shirley Gilbert did what any good manager does in the face of silliness. She told the fellow he was being foolish and got him to back off his demand that we pull the column immediately.

The column stayed up and the new company was named Agilent, which some branding company named for gazillions of dollars. We named it for next to nothing. This was published in March 1999.

A Prune for Your Thoughts

Inspiration leaps out of the most unexpected places sometimes, like a prairie dog popping up in the White House lawn. An article on prunes in a recent edition of the *San Jose Mercury News* yanked my mind out of bed and sent it wandering into the world. The story was too hard to pass, so to speak.

I'll try to share the insights that article inspired in my fully open morning mind, including why California has been such a hotbed of innovation for so many years, why it's such a wacky place to live and the connection between the two.

To reward your indulgence – and to help the realignment effort of Hewlett-Packard Co. and Agilent – we'll kick off a contest that promises a flash of recognition for the winners and some awe-inspiring prizes. Sort of.

Here we go: According to the *Merc's* prune piece, Santa Clara County, California – home to a huge chunk of HP's Bay Area presence – was once the prune capital of the world. In the middle of the past century, close to 60,000 acres of prune orchards dotted the local landscape, bearing thousands of tons of the nutritional nuggets each year.

As local legend goes, an entre-prune-ure named Martin Seely came up with an idea in 1905 to reduce the labor costs of producing prunes. Apparently, Mr. Seely had come across an article about trained monkeys that were used to pick coconuts in the tropics. So he decided to import 500 simians from the jungles of Panama to replace his current prune-pluckers.

"Placed into gangs of 50 each, with a human foreman, the monkeys were set loose into the fields to scamper up the trees," said the article. "The venture was short-lived, however. The monkeys ate the fruit as they picked it, cleaning out his orchard."

Some inspirations turn out better than others, of course. Ideas are like the eggs of loggerhead turtles: The pregnant female lumbers out of the ocean, digs a nest in the sand with her powerful flippers, drops out hundreds of eggs and covers them up to protect them. Most of the eggs hatch, but only a precious few baby turtles survive the predators that line their path between the sand and the safety of the deep blue sea.

For many years, especially in high-technology, California has been the figurative turtle-egg capital of the world. Many of the eggs — in the form of poorly or even well-funded startups — get snarfed up by predators of all kinds. But some grow to magnificent and powerful adulthood: Yahoo!, Google, Hewlett-Packard, Facebook, Apple, Netscape, Disney, Levi's and McDonald's and more. Each one of them was California launched.

But for every tale of the successful audio oscillator, there are hundreds more along the lines of the 500 monkeys — 500 of the most regular monkeys the tree-swinging world has ever seen.

Success and failure. Risk-taking and reward. California and creation. They go together like Romulus and Remus. Antony and Cleopatra. Martha and the Vandellas.

Here's my take on why. I call it the Coffee Filter History of America.

In the late 16th Century, the first European settlers started arriving on the eastern shore of a huge, incredibly fertile country, named for Italian cartographer Amerigo Vespucci. They had embarked on perilous voyages for various reasons: religious freedom, to earn a fabulous living, for the thrill of discovering new lands when it was still an option and to become part of history.

They were innovators, risk-takers, visionaries — along with some mavericks, misfits and a few world-class wackos, too.

After only a few years, some of these early settlers found the relatively civilized confines of the colonies along the Atlantic Coast stultifying: too much structure, too many rules for innovators to follow, not enough room to breathe. So they headed west.

Everywhere they stopped, the same thing happened. After all, these are fiercely independent wanderers who could never quite function in an orderly world, no matter how loose the rules might be. So they packed up again and moved on, searching for something new, something different, something else.

For more than three centuries, these adventurers filtered themselves through 3,000 miles of America, leaving the coarse grounds behind, until a pure 100-proof wave of human java hit the shoreline of the Pacific Ocean on the coast of California.

And there was no place left to go.

Many of them made peace with the physical limitations of the country. They channeled their vast energy into tinkering, inventing, discovering, developing. Some thrived; some didn't; others went crazy.

Most settled in and went to work. And they produced children, many of whom carried the same genetic imprint for questioning the rules, for thumbing their nose at the status quo and who loved to try something new.

Meanwhile, like-minded souls were attracted to this fair-weather state, like the needle of a compass gets tugged to the North Pole. The result? Since the 1800s, California has been up to its Golden Gate in innovation. There seem to be more visionaries per square mile than any other state in the union. They're inventors, artists, scientists, entrepreneurs, producers, engineers. They're the kind of people who have a wild idea in the middle of the night and can't wait until morning to start working on it.

They're also the kind of people who send monkeys into the trees to pick fruit and the ones who laugh the hardest when it doesn't work. Then they ship the monkeys back to Panama and try something even wackier — until they get it wonderfully right.

Now it's your turn to show off your innovation. Wherever you are in the world, you're either a real Californian or an honorary one, thanks to your HP connection. This new measurement company needs an appropriate name. I know we have a fancy consulting company working on it, but who knows this place better than we do?

What do you think the new name should be? Send me your suggestion by the end of this week and I'll post the top five for us to vote on.

Please keep in mind that, big surprise, this is not an official, sanctioned contest. I plan to submit the winning names to the measurement folks, but they could very well reject my overture, which would make this as fruitless as Mr. Sealy's orchard. But let's have some fun anyway.

I have nothing in my prize budget but I have an idea. Top prize will be one pound of home-grown California prunes! Second prize will, of course, be TWO POUNDS of California prunes!

Consider this my way of offering a small token of appreciation to our regular readers, two of whom are destined to be even more regular. So to speak.

Duly Noted: *The top name by popular vote was Addison Technologies, by a near landslide. It reflects the address of the tiny garage where HP was born: 367 Addison Avenue in Palo Alto, California.*

Note: *I had a great relationship with Carly Fiorina in the beginning of her six-year tenure as CEO of Hewlett-Packard Co. (I left the company three years before she did.) She is the most charismatic executive I've ever worked with and possesses a near-photographic memory. And she had a tough job in the beginning – convincing employees to trust this new leader, who was flashy and image-conscious after the humble, soft-spoken-but-tough Lew Platt.*

Right after she started at HP, wild rumors spread about her as you will see. In keeping with our mission of open and honest communication, we decided to address the issue head-on. So I asked Carly if I could use the Apparently So column to have employees submit the rumors they were hearing about her and if I could then interview her to separate the wheat from the sometimes crazy chaff. She agreed and we posted this article in May 2000.

Apparently Not

To paraphrase something the great American humorist Mr. Twain once said, a rumor can travel halfway around the world before the truth has time to lace up its boots. For those of you just joining in, about a month ago, I asked the *Apparently So* faithful to send me all the Carly Fiorina rumors circulating their sites or bouncing about in their email. As always, you folks didn't let me down.

I compiled a list of the five most frequently mentioned rumors (although there were wacky variations on most of them) and turned it into a true-false quiz. I mean, hey, we might as well have some fun with this. So here's the challenge.

Take the following quiz (no peeking at your neighbor's monitor) to determine your Carly Rumor Quotient (CRQ). Simply grab a piece of scrap paper from your recycling bin, write down the numbers 1-5, then put down either True or False after each of the following statements. On your marks. Get set. Go!

1. Carly Fiorina asked the company to add three aircraft to our aviation fleet so she and others could have them available for their global and domestic travel needs.

2. She travels – at company expense – with a personal hairdresser who is from Beverly Hills, California, and wears cowboy boots.

3. Carly ordered the Palo Alto site facilities people to install for her a private, pink-marble executive washroom that includes a shower.

4. Trees were chopped down at the Les Ulis, France, sales office so Carly could land in a helicopter.

5. Her salary is $100 million a year.

BONUS Q: Carly maintains her super-human pace by receiving regular blood transfusions from teen-aged Romanian gymnasts.

OK. Maybe we covered your favorite rumor in there, maybe not. But those were certainly the top nine according to my bulging email bag (I simply couldn't resist sharing the 10th one).

Here is the part that may surprise you. On behalf of my rumor-mongering correspondents out there in HP Land, I asked our president and CEO if she would consider giving me 20 minutes to discuss the top 10 rumors. I told her it might be a valuable use of her time to see if we could put some of the more outrageous ones to rest, and that we could have a bit of fun in the process. She said, "Sure, sounds good."

Last week, I met with Carly and asked her about the veracity of the top 10 rumors. Then I followed up with some additional research. And here we go.

1. Carly Fiorina asked the company to add three aircraft to our aviation fleet so she and others could have them available for their global and domestic travel needs.

True. After talking with Carly last year about how Corporate Aviation could best meet the travel needs of HP's executives, Ken Peartree (head of the organization) sold the company's two Astra APX medium-sized jets and had them replaced with two used Gulfstream IV jets and a used Falcon 50. The Gulfstream IV aircraft are capable of global travel; the Astras were not.

We already owned another Falcon 50 and a De-Havilland twin-otter turbo prop, which runs a weekday shuttle service between San Jose and Roseville, California. So, in total, HP now owns five aircraft.

The twin otter can be used by any HP employee. The other four planes are used by the Executive Council, board members, customers and anybody else who has permission from someone on the Executive Council.

I'm trying to guess the question that lies behind this rumor, but I'm struggling a bit. Carly travels globally more than any other CEO in the history of our company. She squeezes every possible opportunity into every waking moment of her day. For example, on a trip to Colorado in March, she left San Jose in an HP plane at the crack of dawn, flew to Denver, was driven to sites in Fort Collins, Greeley and Loveland where she held meetings and gave site-wide coffee talks, was driven back to Denver where she discussed the state's business climate with the Colorado governor, was driven back to the airport, hopped on the HP plane and was back home by the end of the day.

If she had flown commercial, she'd still be waiting for her luggage.

"These folks use the aircraft to further the business objectives of HP," Ken says. "I think they've clearly been quite successful in keeping the HP name out in front of our customers and the general public, and the availability of our fleet has helped."

2. She travels – at company expense – with a personal hairdresser who is from Beverly Hills, California, and wears cowboy boots.

False. She rolled her eyes and shook her head at this one. "One of the pilots wears cowboy boots," she offered. "But he doesn't do my hair."

3. Carly ordered the Palo Alto site facilities people to install for her a private, pink-marble executive washroom that includes a shower.

False. The things I do for you people. Since there is no substitute for first-hand observation in the journalism game, I took this one on myself. With the help of a female colleague – who shall remain nameless to protect her sterling reputation – I actually entered the facility in question, looking for any trace of hidden powder-room extravagance, including pink marble.

At the appointed hour, my friend met me outside the standard-issue HP bathroom that happens to be the closest to the executive offices. It is used by anybody of the female persuasion within dashing distance. There is, for the record, no such thing as an executive washroom.

My compatriot went inside, looked around and waved me in. With my barely five-foot friend standing menacingly at the door, I burst inside, notebook flailing. I looked left, I looked right, I looked under the stalls. Nothing. No shower. No marble. Nothing you could even remotely call luxurious. It didn't even look as if they had a decent supply of paper towels. In fact, it looked even dingier than the standard issue men's room next door.

Nothing to this one. Case closed.

4. Trees were chopped down at the Les Ulis, France, sales office so Carly could land in a helicopter.

True. This one is my favorite, mostly because I've known this story all along. The rumor started off with a sliver of truth and has since grown into a gnarled, nightmarish oak.

The story: Last October, Carly was traveling through Europe on a typical whirlwind trip. During one day in Paris, her itinerary included the following: an employee breakfast, a Pan-European media conference, individual one-on-one interviews with reporters from four television stations, a roundtable meeting with other journalists, a customer lunch, an employee coffee talk at the Les Ulis office (on the outskirts of Paris) and a dinner for 75 major customers.

One of my delightful European colleagues was responsible for the trip logistics. To try to pack as much as possible into this unbelievably hectic day, he arranged for a helicopter to whisk Carly from a heliport in Paris to the sales office in Les Ulis. It would have been impossible to drive through the congested Paris streets and make the event on schedule.

"At the time, it appeared like a really good idea," says my friend, who shall remain nameless to spare him any further embarrassment.

Unbeknownst to my colleague, Carly doesn't care for two things, despite what some people may think. First, she hates being treated as if she were royalty. Second, she doesn't at all like traveling in helicopters.

When she realized there was no other way to get to Les Ulis in time, she gritted her teeth and jumped on board. The chopper swooped into the air and landed at the site several minutes later.

Unfortunately, there wasn't enough clearance around the facility at the HP site in Les Ulis for the helicopter to land safely. So, in preparing for the visit, a local crew had "dismantled" a half-dozen saplings. The trees were so young they were still held up by wires to keep them from blowing over in a breeze. But they were indeed taken down.

When Carly found out what happened she was, well, let's just say she was unhappy. She made it quite clear the trees were to be replaced and that she didn't want anyone booking her any more helicopter rides in the future.

The funny part is how this rumor morphed over the months. It started off as Carly ordering the trees to be chopped down. Then the site kept moving around. First, the incident happened in France. Then it was Boeblingen, Germany. Then it was in the United States.

Next were the trees themselves. Initially, they were a half-dozen saplings. Then they somehow grew into 100-year-old trees. One message even said that Carly had an entire forest chopped down so she could land. Another had her ordering a private airstrip to be built.

The clincher was a message that said not only had Carly ordered trees to be chopped down, but one of them fell into some power lines, blacking out a large area of France.

The true story: a half-dozen young trees were taken down. Carly did not order this to happen. It was a mistake.

"I am reliably informed," says my dapper friend, "that the trees have been replanted. If not the exact same saplings, some saplings very similar."

5. Her salary is $100 million a year.

False. I'm a bit squeamish on this one, but that's just me. I always thought it was rude to talk about how much money people make, but since everybody wants to know I'll overrule myself.

First, all of this is public information and easily accessible. If you want the details, look at the proxy HP sent out in advance of the annual meeting last February. The details are also in HP's 2000 Annual Report.

Most of Carly's 1999 compensation came in the form of 580,000 shares of restricted stock, which is worth somewhere in the neighborhood of $78 million (U.S.). This compensated her for stock options and grants she left behind at Lucent. She also received 600,000 shares of stock options at a grant price of $113.03 as of July 19, 1999. These vest over four years.

In addition, she received a one-time hiring bonus of $3 million.

So let's separate all that from her salary. Carly's annual base salary is $1 million, plus an incentive bonus of $1.25 million, which is guaranteed. She has the opportunity to earn an additional $2.5 million if certain company goals are met – all based on HP achieving specific aspirational growth in revenue and profit.

Her annual salary, therefore, is $2.25 million, with an upside potential of $4.75 million. The company has to perform and perform well for her to reach the latter figure. Some perspective from HP's manager of Executive Compensation: "Her package is comparable to what CEOs of Carly's caliber could get from other companies this size."

BONUS Q: Carly keeps up her super-human pace by receiving regular blood transfusions from teen-aged Romanian

gymnasts.

False. "They're kidding on that one, right?" she asked. I think so, I told her. I really do think so.

OK. Time to add up your score and figure out your Carly Rumor Quotient (CRQ). Give yourself 10 points for each one you answered correctly, zero points for each one you missed. And here's what your score means:

40-50 points. Philosopher. You don't believe everything you hear. You don't pass on falsehoods. You think before you act. You are trusting, faithful, probably happy with your life. Nice to have you around.

30 points. Doubter. It's normal to feel doubt when your environment is undergoing fundamental changes. There's nothing wrong with it — it's probably even healthy. Just watch that it doesn't slide into the next category.

20 points. Cynic. I can't remember who first said this, but a cynic is a skeptic who has lost all hope. People call me cynical from time to time. I'm not. I wake up each morning filled with hope. On a good day, I still have some left at the end.

0 - 10 points. Hmm. Not sure what in the world to label this. I'm just wondering what rumors you're passing around about *me.*

That's it. I hope you had some fun. I know I did. But I can't let you go without some kind of moral – I guess it's the Aesop in me.

I think it all comes down to this: It's not easy to walk into this company as an outsider, especially when the whole world is watching. One of our collective habits that has both a good and a bad side is our deeply rooted need for conformity. When this means we expect each other to act professionally, uphold our core values, work well together and contribute as a team to something greater than ourselves, it's a wonderful trait.

When it means that it's hard to be different at HP – whether that means looking different, acting differently, thinking in a different way, believing different things – then it can be a problem. We very much need to change this latter part of our need for conformity to live and work in a global era, perhaps more than any of our other bad habits.

And what does Carly think of all this rumor stuff?

"Oh, part of me says it's very predictable and understandable considering all the hype surrounding my appointment to the job," she says. "But there's another piece that doesn't feel so good. I think some people have assumed the worst about me without bothering to investigate. That hurts a little.

"I hope over time that the people of HP and I get to know each other well enough that everyone will know right away that these kind of stories are ridiculous, that they just aren't true."

Her last comments made me think about my own behavior and the phrase "the shining soul of HP" that Carly has used and many of us are struggling to grasp. I've passed along rumors before – not on this topic, but I've done it. Sometimes I've mistrusted people before giving them the benefit of the doubt. I'm not proud of it, but it's true.

For us to get where we need to go as a company, for us to succeed on this journey, we need to trust each other more than we ever have before.

I know it's not a perfect world. Believe me, I know. But let's close with the views of a great French writer, Voltaire. A long time ago he wrote through his character Candide that each of us owns a small piece of the garden and it's our responsibility to tend it.

Note: As I've mentioned, I love all creatures great and small even the gross or dangerous ones. But I realized that I will draw a line when necessary and this line involves whether or not to invite them inside my little house. This article stems from another adventure with my daughter, Ellery. It was written in 2010.

Ants, Abated

My daughter awakened me at 6:15 yesterday morning with the urgent news that we'd been invaded. She grabbed my hand and led me out of the world of dreams while I shook off the cobwebs.

"Look!" she said, after she'd tugged me to the kitchen and turned on the light. "They give me the heebie-jeebies."

There must have been 10,000 Argentine ants on the kitchen counter, their mandibles ripping at the leftover scraps from last night's Safeway-cooked rotisserie chicken. I hadn't cleaned the kitchen the night before, since the dishwasher needed unloading and the couch and a DVR-recorded movie beckoned.

And now a double-column of those busy little insects flowed from the dinner plates and across the counter, over the wall, down the door trim and under the front door, where the foundation had settled, cracking the concrete underpinnings slightly and leaving subterranean paths for the ants to discover.

I grabbed a bottle of Windex from under the kitchen sink and squirted the invaders from the skies, raining napalm onto the troops, killing them before they could scatter. Squirt after squirt of Blue Death washed over the ants, leaving a trail of twisted brown bodies. It looked like the scene in "Jarhead," where the Marines come upon the destroyed buses, trucks and cars filled with the corpses of the fleeing Iraqi Republican Guard. There was nothing left but carbon particles after the Air Force caught up and rained hellfire upon them as they beat a hasty retreat from Kuwait.

All creatures great and small, they say, the Lord God loves them all. Except maybe ants, I think. And wasps and mosquitoes and assholes, great and small. The Lord isn't stupid.

I leave ants alone outside. I know my place. The rule is: Just not where I live. That's where I draw the line.

Although it was now quiet on the Formicidae front, I knew from experience they'd be back. So I threw on some shorts and made the quick trip to Safeway where I perused the various products for annihilating pesky little critters caught in the wrong place at the wrong time. I chose the Grant's Kills Ants box because of its effective packaging with the bold black letters on the red box and the universal circle with the diagonal line across it, indicating that Grant's Obliterates Ants. I paid $7 for a package of 10 ant stakes, with the promise of "destroying entire ant colonies." Oh, the power I now possessed.

I returned home, opened the package and strategically placed four ant stakes on the counter, near the door and at the base of the wall – with the bait hole placed upward, as instructed. The kitchen counter sparkled now, with all traces of the former invading army clinging to wet paper towels in the trash can.

By now, a smattering of scouts had already replaced their sacrificed brethren, purposefully searching and searching, running helter-skelter, hither and yon, until they would bump into another scout, exchange information with their antennae and run off again.

The more I watched these tiny creatures, the more fascinating I found them. They are hard workers, these ants. They can cover a dozen feet of territory on their scurrying little legs in less than a minute and their bodies are only about a tenth of an inch long. That would be like an average-size man searching every nook and cranny of a football field in less than 60 seconds. Try it sometime.

And they communicate to each other not only what they've found through waggling their antennae, but how to get there, too. Amazing.

The new scouts had no interest whatsoever in my Grant's Kills Ants bait. According to the package, they were supposed to discover the bait, eat it, take it back to their nest and feed it to the other ants, including the queen. Then they would all die over the Kool-Aid bowl like Jim Jones and his disciples in the jungles of Guyana, and peace would be restored to my little home.

I took to placing a piece of paper towel in the scouts' path and picking them up when they ran onto it. Then I'd drop them off the paper into the bait hole. They'd jump right back onto their feet, shake themselves and run off – no interest in the bait whatsoever.

After trying to coax at least a dozen of the scouts to nibble some Grant's, I decided they needed further tempting. So I took a couple of tooth picks from the box in my cupboard and stirred the poison bait in the hole of the trap. A chunk of it stuck to the end of the toothpick so I placed the poison in front of a scout, like Salome dancing for John the Baptist, and he actually nibbled a bit. But he hurried off looking none the worse for wear.

After repeating the offer to other scouts, like a doyenne at Trader Joe's, I got a few takers but no one actually took the bait and ran, as promised on the packaging. That was it for Grant's. They had their chance.

I returned to Safeway and this time picked up the Raid Double Control Ant Baits, which were on sale for $4.79 if you had a Safeway card (I do, said the former groom). Their marketing department swore these baits would "Kill the Colony and Keep Killing for 3 Months!" Since we can never have enough killing in this world of ours, I was intrigued.

I took them home, opened the package and placed all four Raid baits on the kitchen counter, near the wall and next to the front door. For good measure, I left out two of the Grant's ant stakes as well and took off to watch my son Owen's Little League baseball game.

He had a respectable outing: He made a great play in the field, got a hit, stole second, danced off the base and his team won by a lot. The only bad part was at the end when all the parents split off from the baseball tribe to go back to their individual tepees. And my children went out for ice cream with my ex-wife. It was her turn, sigh. It still hurts. And I went home to my ants.

I was surprised when I turned on the kitchen light and saw the swarm around my collection of ant baits. The double line of ants – one column coming and one column going – snaked from the door, up the trim, across the short wall and onto the counter. Dozens of ants were inside the Raid traps, gobbling mouthfuls of poison with their jaws. When one ant was satiated, he would leave the trap and join the column marching back to the nest, where he would regurgitate his poisoned dinner for others, including the Queen, to partake. There were even a few ants inside the Grant's Kills Ants baits. The traps had been sprung, the poison ingested – all I had to do now was wait.

This morning, Spencer the Wonder Cat woke me at 7:15, demanding that I stop dreaming about my lottery winnings and the island beach home I now lived in with a trio of the beautiful young women the money attracted. He wanted food. I stumbled out of my room, down the hallway and out into the kitchen. It was quiet.

The traps were empty. The ants were gone.

After a few moments, I noticed a couple of scouts wandering across the counter and down the wall. They must have been the professional athletes of ants, the warriors that are hardest to kill. I went to take a shower and when I came back, not even the scouts were around.

My ants are gone now. Where once there were thousands of those pesky little insects, there is only an expanse of counter top. I feel successful in my quest to rid my home of the invading horde. But I feel hollow, too, as you do when something big is over – whether it's completing a story or a major project at work, moving into a new home or even finalizing your divorce. There's a vacuum, an emptiness, a pool that needs filling.

I miss my ants. And when they come back? I'll watch them for a while, study them, learn from them. Then I'll buy more Raid Double Control Ant Baits. And I'll kill them.

Note: *I dragged my teenage progeny away from their phones and other electronic devices and took them to downtown San Jose for a cultural outing featuring the genius of Leonardo da Vinci. Somehow this story meanders from da Vinci to properly washing your hands to prime numbers and an odd incident in Wales. Go figure.*

Happy Birthday

The other day, my teenage, girl-boy twins (I call them "The Sampler Pack") hurtled into my car, punched the radio to one of the stations they like and we zipped off for a cultural adventure at the Tech Museum of Innovation in San Jose, California.

Fifteen minutes later, I spotted the enormous, bright-red banner hanging from the side of the museum that read: Leonardo: 500 Years into the Future.

For the next couple of hours we wandered through this fascinating exhibit, sucking up the genius of Leonardo da Vinci and some of his Renaissance compadres like a high-powered Wet Vac in a flooded basement.

Not only did these men design some of the most glorious cathedrals in Europe, they also invented the machines to build those stairways to heaven. These enterprising inventors created such useful devices as the screw-operated triple turnbuckle, which sounds like something you'd wear to the Exotic Erotic Ball in San Francisco.

In truth, they used the turnbuckle to lift massive marble columns and other structural elements to erect those magnificent churches.

Despite all the cool gadgets, my favorite display case by far held Leonardo's notebooks. There they were – separated from my eyes only by thick museum glass and air – his actual notebooks and their yellowed pages, crammed with his precise, imaginative drawings.

A sign said that only one-third of his notebooks have survived all those centuries of being carried around in high-school back packs. The ones that exist today are replete with detailed sketches of his inventions, complex studies of anatomy and botany, and ideas for paintings and sculptures.

I can only imagine what the other two-thirds of his notebooks must have contained: blueprints for curing cancer and Alzheimer's disease. Plans for eliminating poverty and other forms of human suffering. A recipe for the perfect Key Lime pie.

Extensive notations in Leonardo's peculiar scrawl accompanied each drawing. I'd already heard about his odd habit of writing left-handed and backwards, as if into a mirror, but when I saw up close his tidy scrawl – which only an Italian pharmacist could read – they imbued me with a sense of awe.

Was he the greatest genius in the history of mankind? An alien from another planet? A human transplanted in time from a future generation?

Even my young teenage children – who have the attention span of a robin's egg – seemed impressed.

After enjoying our cultural fix, the half-gallon of iced tea I'd already imbibed had made its way through the intricate tubing that leads to my bladder and nature screamed for attention. I asked my son if he wanted to come with me to the museum bathroom since pissery loves company.

As I headed for the men's room door with Owen behind me, I dodged the winter sneezing and coughing of the teeming mass of museum visitors. I don't have the world's most robust immune system and I hate getting sick so I'm careful to avoid getting sneezed on, grabbing door handles in public places or even shaking hands if I can do so without insulting someone – especially with all the designer flu craziness going around.

I remembered an article I'd read recently in an online newsletter from my medical clinic. It talked about the importance of hand washing during the cold and flu seasons, and added a useful tip I'd never heard before.

The article said that washing your hands with soap and water wasn't very effective unless you did it vigorously and for at least 20 seconds, which is a long time in this rapidly spinning culture of ours (I live in Northern California's Silicon Valley).

To ensure you scrub enough to receive the most benefit, the article suggested you sing, "Happy Birthday," while washing your hands and to do it twice at a moderate pace. When you finish the second time through, your hands will be sparkling clean and germ-free.

I practiced constantly since reading that article. Every time I washed my hands, I would turn on the faucet to let the water flow, wet my hands, squirt out some liquid soap, turn off the water (we're in a serious drought here in California so we all need to do our part), and then scrub away while I sing the birthday song.

When I got to the dedication part, I would either wish myself happy birthday or whatever three-syllable name popped

into my head. One time it was, "Happy birthday, Kate Hudson."
Another, it was, "Happy Birthday, Dave Matthews."

I was hooked on this new protocol and shared it with my
twins.

In the museum, I hurried into the men's room with Owen
following, snaked my way past the confused gentlemen coming
out the wrong way, reached a urinal and voided the Bota bag of
my bladder. When I finished, I walked over to the wash room.
Out of the corner of my eye, I saw the shape of a tall young man
with light-brown hair and assumed Owen had joined me at the
neighboring sink.

I opened the faucet, tapped on the soap spigot with my fist
and a pink, foamy liquid squirted into my other palm. I started
scrubbing my hands and, comfortable that it was my son beside
me, began to sing in a voice loud enough for him to hear:

"Happy birthday to you,
Happy birthday to you,
Happy birthday, Leonardo,
Happy birthday to you."

I finished the first round with a rousing, baritone "Laaa-la-
la-la-laaa!" and started again.

"Happy birthday to you,
Happy birthday to you,
Happy birthday, Mr. da Vinci,
Happy birthday to you!"

I chuckled to myself and turned to my right to see if Owen was laughing, too. But he wasn't — mostly because it wasn't Owen standing next to me.

Some tall kid I'd never seen before was staring at me with his mouth wide open. He couldn't have looked more startled if I were a topless, purple-haired, eight-foot-tall hermaphrodite standing next to him and singing a carefree version of the birthday song. Or maybe he was just surprised that I squeezed too many syllables into the name slots.

He finished washing his hands quickly and high-tailed it for the safety of the museum floor, water dripping behind him and splashing onto the tile floor. I followed him out — at a safe distance — and shared the story with my kids. It reinforced their teenaged notion that, in fact, their father truly is an idiot.

By this point, we were cultured-out so we walked into the crisp air of a Northern California winter. We found our car and drove back home. Under family rules, it was my turn to pick the music so we listened to Dexter Gordon, Bill Evans and Herbie Hancock during the drive.

As I listened to the jazz tunes, I thought about birthdays and remembered the numerical rule I've developed for them. It goes like this: If your age on your birthday is a prime number (a number wholly divisible only by one or the number itself) or if it's divisible by nine, you're going to have a fantastic year. It doesn't mean the other years will be terrible, but these will be truly special. Try it, because it certainly works for me and those around me.

We drove closer to home and my hand-washing experience at the museum made my mind jump back in time to when I traveled to England and Wales with my kids' mom, who is now my ex-wife (and a good friend, believe it or not). Back then, we flew to London, took a high-speed train to Northern Wales, rented a car and wended our way through the country of my ancestors on a castles and cathedrals tour.

One of our stops was Brecon Beacons, a marvelous national park with rolling green hills dotted with sheep droppings (I strongly believe there are more sheep than humans in Wales). We hiked for hours on a rare sunny day in September and climbed one of the steeper hills.

At the top, we stood on the same spot where my Celtic ancestors lit fires to warn neighboring tribe members that the English army was marching their way, with the intent of inflicting Parliament, Beowulf and Mr. Bean onto the ancient Druid culture of Wales.

After the hike, we came down the hills and headed for the bathrooms at the National Park Visitor Centre. I walked around the building to the men's side and entered a bedroom-sized, rectangular room with an aged concrete floor. I'm guessing it was a changing room, but there were no benches or chairs. An arched doorway beckoned at the far side of the empty room and I assumed it led to the urinals and toilet stalls.

As my eyes adjusted to the darkness, I saw a middle-aged man standing in the corner of the changing room closest to the arched doorway. He was medium-sized, wearing a jaunty pair of bright red suspenders and sporting a well-worn straw hat on his head.

The man's shirt and trousers seemed clean enough but were so wrinkled it looked as though they'd never been ironed since he bought them and perhaps he had slept in them the night before. Hanging from his forearm was the hooked end of a long black cane and he wore a pair of those sunglasses they give you at the eye doctor's office so you can tolerate the sunlight after he dilates your pupils.

This wrinkled fellow smiled gleefully as he sang to himself in the corner. I looked closer and noticed he was also peeing onto the floor. I'm guessing he was either blind or his eyesight was so bad he thought there was a urinal there, but his stream hit nothing but concrete.

As a pool of his urine spread across the floor, seeping around his shoes, the man's smile broadened further until it took up nearly a third of his face – a massive salt-and-pepper moustache bristled across another third.

I had no idea what, if anything, I should do. Should I say something to him? Would that help? Or would it simply spoil his cheerful mood?

Besides, what do you say to a man in another country who's merrily peeing on the floor in the corner of an empty room? It could have been a local custom for all I knew.

So I decided to keep it to myself. I stepped carefully around the flood of pee crossing the floor, past the happy man and into the room with the urinals. I guess I'll never know why he was so cheerful. Maybe it was his birthday.

And it was a prime number.

Note: Sometimes I'm faced with a complex problem I desperately want to solve but have no clue how to approach it. This makes me feel as anxious as a blind crab searching for food in an empty aquarium. Compounding the matter is my lack of confidence at finding a way to break on through to the other side, as the great Jim Morrison once sang. So I end up stuck in a massive, frustrating procrastination loop that can go on as long as Sisyphus rolled that darn rock.

Over my career I've written 10 poems – some of which you might be tempted to call doggerel – and never any others. I wanted to honor these bits of verse with some illustration but have one overwhelming problem when it comes to the graphic arts: I can't draw a bath.

So I made occasional, half-hearted attempts to find someone to illustrate my little bits of rhyme and meter and had zero success. The poems remained stashed on a flash drive year upon year.

Then a serendipitous event occurred when my Higher Power gave me a swift rugby boot to the behind. When the news of my health problems spread to the East Coast, my friend Mike Carr (yes, the great, guitar-slinging dude from the wilds of Virginia) came out west to visit in September 2014 with his lovely wife, Alex, a highly talented graphic artist. We started talking about this book and I asked if she might be interested in illustrating some of the poems. Sure, send them to me and I'll take a look, Alex said.

She did, she volunteered and she did a fabulous job both discerning what in the hazel-eyed world I had in mind with my unusual combinations of words and meanings, and making her illustrations hauntingly beautiful, too. Thank you so much, Alex!

The other bit of serendipity is that I always thought my ex-wife, Mira Dabrowski, would be a terrific person to illustrate the other four. She always drew lovely Xmas cards based on the events of our young family and everyone lucky enough to receive the cards simply adored them. Mira graciously volunteered and applied her lovely, whimsical style to the others. Thank you, Mira!

Procrastination solved – and it only took a decade.

Raining Cats and Doggerel

When I was much younger, I wanted to write children's books. I told myself I would play with the words and make them do tricks while drawing exquisite pen-and-ink sketches that tug the reader into the scene. I'd give my little poems names like "Walking the Doggerel," "Von Braun's Swagger" or "Von Braun's Swagger On a Roll." I'd be just like Shel Silverstein, one of my heroes.

Unfortunately there was a tiny problem: I'm a ridiculously terrible artist. I couldn't draw a lick with a half-tongue head start. Thank goodness I had my good friends Alex Carr and Mira Dabrowski to assist.

And may you forever rest in peace, Shel.

The Hippocratic Oaf

A stethoscope for a stegosaur
Is a silly waste of time.
If he's tickled with a tulip,
He'll tell you that he's fine.

Illustration by Mira Dabrowski

Pecking Order

Little boys chase pigeons,
Keep them pigeons on the run;
Eagles pick up little boys
And eat them just for fun.
Nature watches out
For all the birds that peck and coo;
But I'd rather be an eagle,
Wouldn't you?

Illustration by Alex Carr

Lewis Carolling

"Beware," insists the Jabberwock,
"of things that think
and things that talk,
for one will dig its own abyss
by jesting with paralysis,
the other – thought's antagonist –
rings hollow through the night."

Illustration by Alex Carr

Yowtch!

In histories of the Mid Ages
We read of King Henry's wild rages;
If a word too misleading
Appeared in his reading
He hastily burned all the pages!

Illustration by Alex Carr

First Impressions

The artists rebuke poor René
For finishing one work a day,
Though he often complains
The stigma remains:
He just does it for the Monet.

Illustration by Alex Carr

On Your Honor

Our mayor, Francesco de Yama,
Was casually humping a llama
When an angry vicuña
Said, "Listen here, junior,
You keepa' your hands off my mama!

Illustration by Mira Dabrowski

The Arms of Morpheus

Night time and the masquerade –
a pull from the bottle,
a tug on the shade,
Uncluttered heroes
Performing fantastical,
Flittering follies
Elusive, elastical,
Galwags galumphing
Triads triumphing
Perusing the pounce
Of a cameo cat
While the fire, unrehearsed
Blows a flickering scat:
Zum-ba-da-doo
ba-da-voo
ba-da-zee;
Then comes the morning –
The much dreaded morning –
When I awake
With nothing but me.

Illustration by Alex Carr

Don't Be Cilia

I have a paramecium
I went and named him "Bud"
He loves to hike
And roller skate
And wrestle germs for fun.
He even knows a special trick
My paramecium
Cause every time
I call his name
He makes another one!

Illustration by Mira Dabrowski

Assailing, Assailing

"Sargasso, seize the scallops,"
Cried the cruller captain's crew,
"Hustle in the mussels
And we'll pop them in the stew."

"Alba, core the albatross
And grind his bones for tea,
For the Prince of Wales
Has left his post
And joined us out at sea."

Illustration by Alex Carr

Endless Lub

I love your Bolivian olives, Olivia,
But you leveled my love when you
Left me for Libya;
Your lyrical lapse
Has pickled my paps
And shaken me, top hat to tibia.

Illustration by Mira Dabrowski

Note: When we were dating long distance between Caxias do Sul in Brazil and Mountain View in California, Fátima asked me if I had ever written a Christmas story. I hadn't, but kept her idea in my mind. And this is what finally emerged from those crevasses, in December 2008.

Let There Be Lights

Yesterday I finally got around to putting up my six-foot strand of blue outdoor Christmas lights. Every foot or so, I tied the covered wires with string to attach them to the top of the banister surrounding the porch of my modest manufactured home. This way, the lights can dangle like icicles of varying length.

Since I hate to plug in Christmas lights every sunset and then streak outside in my evening attire (a hoodie and microbriefs) near midnight to unplug them, I bought a light-sensitive timer for only $7.99. This nifty device promised to turn on my lights as the sun set and switch them off again seven hours later (or any number of hours I wanted to program).

It was the best almost-eight-dollars I ever spent. I praised the engineers who designed and manufactured such a useful gadget as I plugged the timer into the outlet. Then I stood and admired my work for about 20 minutes – as all men do when they finish a project around the house.

I love blue lights for Christmas. They're beautiful, elegant and subtle – a flicker of simplicity in our over-wrought western world.

Most of the people on my street who intended to put up lights had already done so. Their bulbs were red and green, sometimes with a touch of orange and yellow.

"Your neighbors are going to think yours are for Hanukkah," my daughter Ellery said.

"Maybe so," I chuckled.

That was fine by me. Perhaps I was celebrating both holidays in my mind, embracing the radical concept of peace on earth among multiple religions.

About three years after our divorce, my ex-wife was traveling to attend a seminar, so I had our 14-year-old twins to myself.

I adore everything about having my children around all the time, except for the transition. As a rule, those of us who possess the Y chromosome do not handle transitions very easily. It's mostly because we're simple creatures who can only focus on one thing at a time. The basic circuitry of a man is wired like a 9-volt battery to a refrigerator light bulb.

Transitions require flexibility, a penchant for multi-tasking and the mental ability to keep plates spinning on poles while juggling a dozen eggs. Women do this all the time and are adept at it. Too many neurons stimulated at once overheat a man's simple circuitry and he typically pouts in frustration or barks in anger.

I'm working hard on transitions these days, using the tools I've learned to soften the hard edge: deep breathing, meditating, half-smiling (something I discovered in a

Dialectical Behavioral Therapy class). I breathe in (1, 2, 3, 4) and out (1, 2, 3, 4) and keep increasing the numbers until I reach nine.

And somewhere a choir of angels sing:

"It came upon a midnight clear,
That glorious time of old."

It's the rapid creep into rush hour now, as I pick up the kids from school. They're both hungry but my son, Owen, remembers that he needs a book from the library so he can work on the English project due Thursday.

So we head over to where they live with their mom. We drop off Ellery so she can get a snack and a head start on her own homework, and Owen and I zip over to the Sunnyvale Pubic Library to see if we can temporarily acquire one of their copies of "Black Hawk Down."

My son brings up the library's in-house computer and clacks in the title. The screen tells us one copy is "In Mending" and the other is on a nightstand in somebody else's home.

Darn it. So I use my charm on the twenty-something librarian's assistant and discover all too quickly that my charm is about 20 years overdue.

She finds us a copy anyway – at the Mountain View Public Library, which is three miles away through the darkening crawl of flashing lights and darting bicycles. About 12 minutes later, we arrive unscathed and ease into the library's Lilliputian parking lot.

Owen and I walk inside and up to the main desk where we're met by a six-foot-two, 130-pound, pretzel rod of a young man.

"The Sunnyvale library says you have a copy of 'Black Hawk Down,'" I venture. "Can you find it, please?"

The sparsely bearded fellow clickety clacks on the keyboard and peers at the screen.

"Yes," he says. "One's been returned. Can I see your library card?"

"I don't have one," I reply. "But I live in Mountain View. Can I get one?"

"I need to see your driver's license or other proof of residency," he repeats in a practiced voice with all the emotion of a praying mantis.

I show him my license but it still has the address of the kids' house on it. It's been almost four years since I moved out and I still haven't gotten around to changing it.

"Do you have something with your current address?" the praying mantis inquires.

I think for a moment, rifling through all the file cabinets in my brain, but slower and less effectively than even a few years ago.

"Yes!" I remember. "I have an insurance card in my car. I'll have to go get it."

*"From angels bending near the earth
To touch their harps of gold."*

I hurry outside because that's the way I am and power walk the block to my car. I need to get there and back before some other citizen swoops in and snatches the last existing copy of "Black Hawk Down." I can't disappoint my son. I just can't.

I unlock the car, open the door and reach into the glove compartment. Amid the napkins, the bottle of Tums, watermelon-flavored sugarless gum and assorted important papers, I find the insurance card with my new address. I hustle back inside.

There are now five people in the line to talk to the fellow I left about five minutes ago. Where did they all come from? People can be like ants and the world is a dropped peanut-butter-and-jelly sandwich.

I want to patent a bumper sticker and sell it online and in gift shops around the world in various languages. It will have that shouting figure from the Edvard Munch painting on a white background and these words screaming in black:

"People – they're everywhere!"

I wait in line with Owen as patiently as a Type-A male can, trying to calm my heart, which is pounding like it's underneath Edgar Allan Poe's floorboards. I wonder if I should go straight to the front of the line since I've already been there. I weigh my sense of entitlement against my sense of civility.

Civility tips the scales – but only by the weight of a hummingbird's wings – and we wait.

When it's finally our turn, I show the man the insurance card. He completes the necessary administrivia and hands me the precious Mountain View Library Card – the horse-hoof boat my son and I can ride across the River Styx and into literary heaven.

The young fellow walks into the room behind him and comes out a few minutes later – with Bach trumpets blaring and the cherubim singing – with a bedraggled copy of "Black Hawk Down."

The angelic choir shouts triumphantly:

"Hallelujah!"

We drive back to the kids' house through an angry snarl of people running happy holiday errands or limping home after another 12 hours of high-tech or biopharmaceutical or some other kind of work. As the great Canadian-born poet Joni Mitchell once sang: "I can see it out in traffic – everyone hates everyone."

We reach the house and pick up Ellery. I'm crabby from another hectic day at work, the libraries, the traffic and all the people. She is my mood ring, my reflection in a clear pool of water. Ellery doesn't care for transitions either. She is a lovely girl in so many ways but her nervous system can overload easily when she's with her family and feels safe enough to act out.

We are so alike. Children are indeed nature's revenge.

By the time we turn into the street that leads to my house, the darkness has swallowed us. I'm hoping the cheerful sight of my blue Christmas lights will nudge me back into the spirit of this glorious holiday:

"Peace on the earth, goodwill toward men,

From heaven's all gracious king."

As we move slowly down my narrow block, every other place greets us with glowing lights from the Christmas palette. We roll toward my house, a few spaces up on the left. In my mind, I see six glorious feet of elegant blue icicles shining steadfastly through the black of night, a beacon leading us through the dark.

We drive past Tom's place. Then Suzette's home. Then Kate's. One more to go. We're almost there. We're almost there!

We edge past the last place next door and can finally see my humble home. And it's completely dark. No lights. No beacon. No warm electric greeting.

I mutter my disappointment to myself in a word I rarely use around the children. Ellery can't understand what I said and asks me to repeat it as I park the car.

"Never mind," I say.

"What?" she repeats.

"Never mind," I bark.

As soon as the words leave my lips, I deeply regret having said them, especially with that volume and that tone of voice. Ellery, my mirror, storms out of the car, slams the door and walks off. Owen gets out more quietly and is enveloped by darkness.

Darn it. I'd let the stress of my day and the chores and the rush-hour traffic and my disappointment get to me. I know better than that. I don't want my kids growing up and repeating the same practice with their kids. I just forgot to use my tools. Darn it.

Apparently So

I decide to let Ellery cool off before I apologize to her, before I hug her and tell her humbly and from the heart how much I love her. After so many years of stunted emotional growth and the newness of sobriety, I'm still learning how to be an adult, how to be sane, how to be wise.

I sit in my car under the carport roof and breathe deeply, centering myself. Owen appears out of the darkness and taps on my window. I open the door and get out.

"Father," he says. (I don't know why, but he's chosen to call me "Father.") "Let me show you something."

We walk toward the front of the house and around the carport corner. When we reach the front, it's glowing brilliantly with those beautiful, soothing blue lights.

Owen leads me around to the other side of the house, where the electrical outlet juts from the wall.

"The lights work a whole lot better when you plug them in," he says.

Oh, my. In my haste to finish the job, I had neglected to plug the outdoor extension cord into the timer.

"So they do, my son," I answer, laughing out loud at my error. "So they do."

I hug him and breathe deeply again, this time inhaling the winter chill along with the essence of the season glowing from those soft blue lights. I hold the breath as long as I can and then release it, blowing out the darkness from within me:

> *"The world in solemn stillness lay*
> *To hear the angels sing."*

And this time I do hear them – clearly, convincingly – their voices traveling great distances through the cold night air. It's been years and years, but once again, as I hug one child and prepare to embrace the other, I can hear the angels sing.

Note: *Here's a story first published in Tieline East after my initial trip to HP Corporate Headquarters in Palo Alto. It later ran in Jay Coleman's publication MEASURE, which served the entire company and won many professional awards before its budget was eliminated in 2000. The tale is about my chance encounter with Bill Hewlett, simply a brilliant, lovely man (and I can say the same thing about Jay Coleman!).*

The Man and the Myth

You can praise my ancestors and call it the luck of the Welsh if you like. Or kismet. Or blind chance. Or serendipity.

Whatever you call it, the gods handed me a healthy dose the day I met Bill Hewlett, co-founder of Hewlett-Packard Company.

Way back in 1988 I ventured to Palo Alto, California, from my Rockville, Maryland, office to take part in the annual gathering of HP communicators from around the world. It was near the end of my rookie year at HP and I asked a young man named Vernon, who worked in Corporate Communications, if he would give me a tour of the company's historic monuments, which are scattered throughout this lovely Bay Area town.

Our first stop was the garage itself, that familiar icon at 367 Addison Avenue, which became the centerpiece of the HP reinvention campaign in the early years of this millennium. As we pulled up in front of the modest structure, Vernon explained that it's only a good 5-iron shot from Stanford

University, where HP co-founders Bill Hewlett and David Packard attended classes with their professor and mentor, Fred Terman.

Fred started one of the most enchanting myths in high-tech history. "If the car was in the garage, there was no backlog," he had said, referring to the original Silicon Valley start-up, which consisted of a small house they rented along with a driveway and small garage. "But if the car was parked in the driveway, business was good."

Vernon told me a reporter for an industry trade publication was writing a story on the early years of HP. The reporter had asked a reasonable question: Whose car was it?

The conventional thinking leaned toward Dave's 1936 Chevy, but nobody was sure. With this tidbit floating in the back of my mind, we continued our tour, past the Tinkerbell Woodshop nestled between Polly and Jake's antique store on El Camino Real (both of which are gone today). Then we moved on to the Redwood Building a block away, which was the corporate headquarters in 1948 and the initial home of Agilent Technologies after the company split into the computing and printing business in one company (HP) and the test and measurement business in the other (Agilent).

Finally, we drove west, up Page Mill Road to HP Labs where – at the time – Bill and Dave still kept tabs on the global empire they had created.

Vernon and I walked through the distinctive building with the saw-tooth roof, pausing in front of the wood-paneled offices of the founders. That's when the luck kicked in.

By chance, Bill was there, talking in his office with a small group of visitors from Japan. The meeting was breaking up, and the guests thanked him for his time. Bill walked out with them, stopping to talk with Molly Yoshizumi, his executive assistant.

Vernon nudged me.

"Why don't I introduce you?" he said.

Never one to mess with serendipity, I nodded and followed him over.

A moment later, we shook hands, this humble communications scribe from the East Coast and the great man himself. I remember being pleasantly surprised at how tan and fit Bill looked for a man who had 75 years of living behind him at the time. Most impressive were his eyes – there was a benevolent, dancing sparkle within them, one that spoke of wisdom, contentment and even a hint of mischief.

With his body language, Bill invited us to join his chat with Molly. I realized he was trying to recall whose car was parked in the driveway.

"I had a Dodge back then," he said, "but it didn't have a backseat. It was cheaper that way."

I asked if he was referring to the Terman myth. He smiled.

"I don't know how that story got started," he said. "We didn't use the garage for the car. We worked there. I think there was even a power meter in the middle of it. But it's a good story."

He paused for a few seconds, then laughed.

"Tell them it was Packard's Chevy," he chuckled. "We'll let him be the liar."

Call it luck, I guess. That seems to fit best. Whatever you call it, I was there the day Bill added his gentle touch to the myth of the car in the driveway.

The real story won't change a thing, of course. That's because one of the many endearing things about myths is this: The good ones will outlive us all.

Note: *I love to visit Manhattan for a few days to see a play or musical, hear some fabulous music, savor the delicious food and take in the electric, eclectic, eccentric nature of the town. This one starts with a cab ride with dear friends and moves on to an encounter with a hostile cat, named Ceci.*

A Beer and a Slice

I was riding shotgun through the streets of Manhattan in a shiny new taxi one early spring night. My dear mentor Shirley Gilbert sat in back next to her daughter, Lisa, who doubled as my pal. When Lisa smiled, you could easily imagine Meg Ryan.

Shirley and I had been working on a Carly Fiorina all-employee webcast scheduled to go live the next morning with a local audience of about 300 Hewlett-Packard employees from the city.

The dry run had gone well; every word in the slides had been debated, vetted and finally approved; and the production crew was occupied with its last preparations. Although it was rare to be finished this far ahead of a show, there was nothing left to fret over. So Shirley and I decided to go out for a great Manhattan meal with Lisa, who, ironically, worked for IBM locally.

As traffic paused uptown on 5th Avenue, a young woman – who would have been pretty if she had washed her hair and face – stood on the sidewalk yelling at an equally disheveled and out-of-shape young man.

"No, I DIDN'T!" she hollered at him, swaying like a bath towel draped over a worn clothesline on a breezy day at the beach. "I most surely DID FUCKING NOT!"

Ah, another debutante out to take the evening air. She held a bottle of Old Somebody or Other in her left hand and looked as if she were ready to pop him one with her coiled right. As for the male half of this happy couple, he was having none of her carefully reasoned argument. He leaned heavily against the side of a building, shaking his head yes, yes, yes, you most surely fucking did.

Then the traffic picked up and we slowly left them to stumble through the rest of the evening, stretched out unsteadily before them.

"Alcohol," said Lisa, with the tone and cadence of a TV announcer, "the great social lubricant."

Indeed it is. Are you feeling down? Tired? Unsure of yourself? Nervous around other people? Just do what I do. Pour yourself a shot of Jack Daniels over ice. Or you can use Scotch, if you prefer. Or gin, vodka, vermouth, cognac, brandy. Doesn't matter – it all works. How about a glass of white wine? Or a red? Or maybe even a beer. It can be imported, domestic – that's the magic of alcohol – any kind can do the trick.

Just slide the liquid down your throat. It will hit that spot immediately – that hole in your self-confidence that's been there since you were young. That lack of love and attention.

That lack of self-esteem. That lack of courage. That flaw that's part genetic, part behavioral.

Yes, indeed. Step right up and get your alcohol! You don't have to be that person you despise. Get rid of that shy, nervous, awkward character. Turn yourself into the witty, charming raconteur that everyone loves and you love to be.

Yes, the life of the party! You can be that person. It's easy! Just open your mouth and have a drink. And if one makes you feel better so fast, so easily, have another. And another. And another.

You're smart now. You're handsome. You're beautiful. You're courageous. You're all the things you want to be. Ah, yes. Alcohol will tell you anything to keep you drinking.

I didn't stand on street corners brawling with girlfriends, but I did something similar once. Years earlier, I was living with my then-wife in Arlington, Virginia. We had adopted a cat, Ceci, who was born in the heating ducts of the Dancing Crab restaurant in Northwest D.C., where my former sister-in-law, Kris, worked. A stray mama cat had dropped a litter in the only warm, dry place she could find.

The restaurant manager discovered the kitty crèche not long after the young ones had been licked clean. He threatened to drown "every last one of them." So Kris, who's even more of a bleeding heart animal lover than I am, took the six kittens to her crowded Maryland townhome and tried to find homes for them all. We helped her out by taking Ceci, even though we already had a pair of cats.

Once we got her home, I did everything for Ceci. I fed her twice a day, brushed her regularly, clipped her nails, took her to the vet for her shots and check-ups, scooped her litter box daily, built her a cat door so she could go in and out. You know what she did for me in return? Pretty much nothing.

Ceci adored my former wife, who did very little as far as regular feline maintenance goes. It didn't matter to Ceci – she would leap into Mira's lap as soon as she sat down. Ceci would follow her around the house, rubbing up against her legs.

Whenever I got close to Ceci, she would either walk away with a flick of her tail and that look cats can give you – full of haughty disdain. Or she would raise her back and hiss at me like a cornered Canada goose.

So I had a huge, simmering resentment against this feline freeloader. One weekend day when I was alone in the house with Ceci and the other cats, I was two or three sheets to the wind. This was before we had kids so I was drinking Heineken.

I swaggered into the small living room of our Cape Cod house in Arlington, Virginia. On the side of the room facing the street, we had a bay window with ferns and other plants looking out onto the neighborhood. We had placed a three-story, carpeted cat stand that I had built in front of the window so that whichever cat was on top – usually Ceci since she dominated the other, larger cats – could enjoy the view. With my contact lenses in (I thought glasses were too cumbersome when wearing them to take photos, part of my job, so I switched), I could see the detail of the flora outside, with the green lawns, plants and trees of the neighborhood. When the rhododendrons and azaleas were in bloom, it was quite pretty.

And there was Ceci, hunkered down onto the top platform of the cat stand. I approached her, thinking maybe I'd try to make peace on this lovely day and pet her. As I got a few feet away, she looked at me. Then she turned away and hissed.

Now I had taken her disdain for years up to this point and I was instantly sick of it. My desire to pet her melted away like the Wicked Witch of the West and all I had left was a burning hatred of that particular animal, which was so out of character for me. I adored animals. I'd even worked in a cat shelter in Colorado for a time, nursing sick kitties back to health – feeding them through tubes in their necks – and cleaning up after the healthy ones. But I had alcohol in me now and this cat had crossed a line.

"Screw you, you stupid cat," I said.

And I know how ridiculous this is going to sound, but I began stalking her like a middleweight mixed martial arts fighter, my hands open, bobbing and weaving toward her.

"You want some of me?" I barked at her. "C'mon, Ceci, let's go!"

So here I am, talking to a cat, ready to swing at her and doing it in full view of the neighborhood. Ah, yes, the many glorious benefits of alcohol, the social lubricant.

I swatted at Ceci, missing her head by a few inches, trying to scare her. She flinched slightly but mostly just stared at me with those angry green eyes.

I bounced in place for a moment, then side to side and moved in for the attack. I'm not sure what I had in mind – maybe just to swat her once and show her who ruled this animal kingdom.

As I moved toward her, she responded with the speed of a hooded cobra that senses more than sees an opening to attack the stalking mongoose. Ceci's right paw, claws extended, swiped at my eyes with the intent of gouging them out. She returned to her feral state where wild cats rake at the eyes of their foes, trying to blind them. I felt her attack coming before I saw it and I tried to snap my head back as fast as I could.

I saw the blur of her paw pass by my left eye as I leaned backward. The shock of her attack and her going for my precious eyes took the fight right out of me. I looked at her and she stared back, poised, ready to launch another kitty missile.

I stepped back and she looked fuzzy to me, out of focus. I blinked my eyes and she looked like a mass of steel grey fur, instead of the sleek, short-haired kitty she was.

I could see she was squatting on her haunches now. She knew the fight was over and that she'd won. I took a step toward her and by squinting I could see there was something glistening, reflecting light on the end of her paw. I took another step forward and saw what it was: At the end of an extended claw on her right paw dangled my left contact lens.

She had taken the lens right out of my eye with the swipe of her claws. I imagined what would have happened if I hadn't snapped my head back. She would have raked her claw right across my eye.

I never tried to mess with Ceci again, although I did continue to drink, for 15 more years. It's a hard habit to break when the imagined relief alcohol gives still outweighs the real-life pain it causes. And I had a long way to go before reaching the stage of accrued consequences.

Years later, I went in for my annual eye exam with a new optometrist. He examined my eyes, pronounced them fit. However, he said, there's this long faint scratch across your left eye.

"Did you injure it somehow?" he asked.

Yeah, I thought. I guess I did.

"I was breaking up a catfight," I told him. "It probably wouldn't have happened but one of them was drunk."

He just looked at me – with both of his clear, unmarked eyes. And he didn't say a thing.

Note: A classic family story about Poppy, my maternal grandfather, and his adventures on the roads more than 50 years ago, leads into some great advice for living from David Packard, co-founder of Hewlett-Packard Company.

Bastards

A classic story from my mother's side of the family features my grandfather, who we loved dearly and called "Poppy." I knew him best when he was in his 70s and I was a teenager. Poppy was left-handed, laugh-out-loud funny and swore like a Major League manager who just slammed a drawer on his thumb.

Twenty years after his death, he remains one of my major influences.

One Saturday afternoon long ago, Poppy took my five-year-old cousin Mark out for a drive. They came home about three hours later. Nana, my equally beloved grandmother, asked Mark how the drive was.

"Oh, it was fine," said Mark in his little boy voice. "But there sure were a lot of bastards on the road."

I still laugh about it today. And some days I completely understand what Poppy was talking about, especially when someone goes raging through a red light about five seconds after it's changed from yellow. On those days I wonder about this species of ours. I wonder why life is so short but ignorance seems to go on forever.

And it's always the little things that make me crazy – the ones I should be able to calmly accept. I can't even contemplate the big issues: Iraq, Darfur, the homeless, why manufacturers make products that are easy to discard by the people who use them but are unable to quickly biodegrade.

Here's an example of the stuff I question. This used to happen all the time when I ate lunch at the Hewlett-Packard cafeterias, both in Palo Alto and at Cupertino. You stand in the line for the soup of the day, waiting as patiently as a heavily caffeinated Type A can. And the guy in front of me starts doing it.

With the ladle clutched in his talon-shaped hand, he scoops way down into the bottom of the soup cauldron, like a pelican dipping $5,000 koi from a bucket. He pulls out a mother lode of noodles, vegetables, chicken – and plops the cargo into his bowl. Then he does it again. And again. Right before my unbelieving eyes.

This Selfish Soup Scooper was repeatedly committing the most grating breach of public soup etiquette possible. And making a triple "S" of himself in the process.

When he finished his plundering, the stack of food in his bowl climbed above the thimbleful of liquid like a volcano rising from an atoll in the Pacific.

The bad angel on my shoulder heckled the man, shouting all the things I dearly wanted to say.

"Hey, Pal," he barked. "Don't you need a flag for that? We don't want planes flying into it."

But the good angel on my other shoulder just sighed. I knew I wouldn't say anything. It was one of those situations I'm just supposed to accept.

I hate moments like that. In those situation, I wish I could turn into somebody super-manly, like Russell Crowe. He would stand in front of the man and coolly point out the oaf's selfishness in a way that preserved the dignity of both of them. And he'd have a little power on his side – just in case the fellow needed a bit more convincing.

Unfortunately, if they ever make a movie out of my life, I'll probably get Billy Bob Thornton – plus 15 pounds.

For the real me, it's especially hard to be cool in situations like that, when my testosterone is pounding my plowshare into the biggest damn sword it can get its hands on. What I wanted to say was, "Excuse me, but there is a limited amount of soup and there are many of us in the line. If you stir up the whole pot and scoop from there, everyone will have enough."

To which he would graciously reply, "Oh, yes, dear sir. I see the error of my ways. Thank you so very much for pointing them out."

Or Plan B where he shoves the ladle up my nose.

In all honesty, I'm troubled both by the Soup Scooper and my own belligerent reaction to it. The great Dave Packard, co-founder of Hewlett-Packard Company, addressed the difficulty of dealing with other people quite eloquently more than a half-century ago –back in 1958. I ask that you please forgive the gender-specific language – I don't feel right updating his words for our politically correct times.

At HP's second management meeting in Sonoma, California, Dave offered his 11 simple rules for working and living.

"Think first of the other fellow," was at the top of the list. "This is THE foundation – the first requisite – for getting along with others," he said. "And it is the one truly difficult accomplishment you must make. Gaining this, the rest will be a breeze."

Great sentiment, Mr. Packard. But it was hard to accomplish in the slower times of last century, when Americans actually made things. Today we import most of what we buy. We have an enormous trade deficit. We can't balance our budget. We're trillions of dollars in debt. We're over-booked, running late, gotta be somewhere else. As a country, we seem to have no idea where we're going and we're in an enormous hurry to get there.

My fear is that we're falling apart before our eyes, before our children have a chance to enjoy the freedom our forefathers and mothers fought to save. And lest you think I'm overreacting – that you're watching a once-promising mind unravel like a 10-dollar sweater in a coin-operated washing machine – it's not going to happen with a cataclysmic bang. It's going to happen inch by inch, step by step, red light by red light, decision by decision.

Yes, indeed, my friends – it's going to happen ladle by ladle.

Note: *Unfortunately, I have been unable to hold my tongue when a natural set-up line is floated like a basketball over the rim. I slam it through the hoop with relish, never worrying about the consequences. Here are a couple of occasions when the force of justice hit swiftly and hard.*

Dumbstruck

I've only been clobbered by a woman twice in my life. Each time it was triggered by – surprise, surprise – something I said.

Some years ago, I was having what's left of my hair cut by Stephanie James. She's a dear friend and I've been going to her since I moved to California's Bay Area, back when pterodactyls soared over the valley instead of turkey vultures.

One day, Stephanie and I were deep in snip n' gab when an older woman, maybe in her early 80s, toddled over and interrupted us. With a thick Viennese accent, she told Stephanie to stop what she was doing and scribble down a new appointment in The Book. Without so much as a nod to her breach of etiquette, the woman insisted that she simply – right this very moment – had to have Stephanie make an appointment to color her hair.

So Stephanie dutifully moved away from me and reached for The Book.

"You're the only one I want for color," the older woman announced loudly to the entire salon. "I don't care who blows me."

With the timing and cadence of a young David Letterman, I replied, "You know, I'm exactly the same."

Everybody in the salon choked back guffaws – except Stephanie, who, unfortunately for me, had been dutifully attending kickboxing classes for the past eight months.

With the elderly woman completely oblivious to what I'd said, Stephanie whirled from The Book with the speed of Jackie Chan on crystal meth and kicked me hard in my upper left leg. I gulped in my laughter as the greyhounds of pain raced up and down my nervous system.

While Stephanie turned back to the woman, I scrubbed my thigh, trying hard to call off the dogs.

Despite the Swift Foot of Retribution, I decided it was worth it. When someone tosses you the ball that far over the rim, you slam it through. You can't worry about who or what you might land on.

The incident at Stephanie's was the second time I was struck dumb by a woman. The first occurred much earlier, when our twins were just under three years old. My now ex-wife, Mira, and our kids were at the home of Tom and Rose, some wonderful friends who lived in Herndon, Virginia. They're divorced now, too. Heavy sigh.

It was a typically raucous dinner party with four or five families, several with young children. Everyone conversed happily as the adults swilled two or 12 cherry sodas or their equivalents – or maybe that was just me back then.

Late in the evening, a half-dozen kids roared around the family room in front of Tom and Rose's massive big-screen TV. Most of the adults stood and continued their amiable chatter. Mira had just changed our daughter Ellery's diaper in the bathroom. Somehow Ellery had pulled off a successful prison break and she streaked naked into the room.

My young daughter ran right in front of the big-screen TV and started a wild tribal dance to her own music. As she twirled in the nude in front of the room, Mark and Linda's seven-year-old son, Thomas, stared at her. Then he pointed and shouted excitedly: "Look, that kid doesn't have a penis!"

We all laughed. When the waves of laughter broke on the sands and reached up onto the beach, in the brief moment of silence that follows, I replied, "With what she has, she can have all the penises she wants."

Mira turned and whacked me hard on the shoulder, something entirely out of character for her. Maybe it was an early warning sign.

The next morning, the anesthetizing effect of alcohol had dissipated but my shoulder was still sore.

The world received its first warning about my peculiar ability to zing hard, fast and off-color when I was in elementary school. Although I always received high grades, my teachers often marked a particular box under the "Citizenship" section on the back. That box shouted: "Lacks Self Control."

I thought they marked it because I was funnier than they were and they wanted to get even. Now I realize that my speedy knack for verbal word association, often at the expense of others, is a character flaw. Where once I thought it was a gift, today I'm almost certain it's more like a mild case of Tourette's syndrome.

Either way, it's important to note that no good line goes unpunished. In fact, when our twins were in elementary school a few years back, our lovely male child, Owen, came home with an excellent report card: Straight A's read the academic box score. Except for... Uh oh. What's this? A checkmark next to the modern-day euphemism for "Lacks self-control."

Oh, no. As I reflected, I reminded myself of one of the most useful lessons I've ever learned from my genetic replacements. I've said it before and I'll say it again: Children – they're nature's revenge.

Note: Confusion reigned in Hewlett-Packard when email intended for me started going to another David Price. By the time I researched this article, the number had ballooned to five David Prices in the company. I asked a friendly IT fellow to do some research for me and this column includes the results of who really had it worst at the name game. This was written back in 1999.

Beside Myself

Today I just wanted to strangle myself. Again and again and again.

Throughout my life, it's been a minor inconvenience, like a bug splat on an otherwise clean windshield. But as the years have gone by, it's only gotten worse. So bad, in fact, that now my windshield looks like I just drove 80 miles an hour through a swarming cloud of stink bugs.

Let's back up a bit and you'll see why this situation has twisted my colon into a granny knot.

In 1987, I joined Hewlett-Packard Company as an eager young recruit. That was the Stone Age of electronic communication, but even then HP had a proprietary e-mail network called HP Desk.

Shortly after I began – full of energy, full of promise – I got a call.

"Missed you at the meeting," a colleague said.

Meeting? What meeting?

"This morning," she continued. "It was on internal communication strategy. I thought you'd be there."

Well, sure, that makes sense. That's a natural assumption. It is, after all, my job!

"I never heard about it," I said.

Now, I'm as obsessive-compulsive as all the other HP employees (we always hire people just like ourselves). I don't miss meetings, I tie up loose ends, I respond to voicemail as soon as the blinking red light goes on. I even dust my monitor once a week with a soft, lint-free cloth. So trust me when I say I DON'T MISS MEETINGS.

At least the ones I know about. Hmm... The ones I know about.

The clue drove me to my keyboard and I clickety-clacked a short message into our e-mail system and tried to address it to myself. Two names came up:

David Price, Boise, Idaho

David Price, Rockville, Maryland

The second one was me. The first one, the default, was my doppelganger, my imposter, my nemesis.

So I sent him a note. I told him I had recently joined the company, we shared the same name and it would be great if he forwarded any messages that clearly weren't intended for him. And I would do the same.

He seemed nice enough. Sometimes he forwarded messages to me, sometimes he didn't. As it turns out, he was more annoyed than I was about people sending him errant messages.

He went to his local system administrator and had the person add his middle initial to his name to, in his mind, lessen the chances of someone sending the message to the wrong David Price. A week or so after we talked the first time, I addressed a message to myself. My counterpart in Boise was now David L. Price.

I know it's hard to believe the coincidence, but guess what my middle initial is? Yes, it is also "L," short for "Lewis" (the Welsh spelling). I didn't have the heart to tell him.

Once the DLP in Boise gave me a call. He said he had received some photos in the mail and asked if I wanted them. I replied that it depended on what they were.

"One has a lady sitting on a cow," he said.

I asked him to please send them to me and he complied. When the delivery arrived, I opened it and looked at the photo he had described. It was a shot of Lucile Packard, the world-renowned philanthropist and wife of David Packard, company co-founder along with Bill Hewlett. And she wasn't sitting on a cow. It was a lovely horse. I thought everybody in Idaho knew the difference between a cow and a horse. So much for assumptions.

The situation got worse as my corporate life continued. At one point in my time at HP, after several mergers and acquisitions, there were five David Price's in the company. I thought that was horrible until I did some research and discovered there were 26 David Smith's in HP. Two of them even worked in the same city, in the same laboratory, in the same department and for the same manager. As usual, my problem was nothing compared to somebody else's.

The best part about this is the interesting tangential things you discover when you research something, which explains my fondness for a physical dictionary as well as an online spelling and definition tool – one for depth and serendipitous connections, the other for speed.

As it turns out, there were three Wayne Scott's in the HP directory. These gentlemen worked in different parts of the U.S. and kept in regular contact. When all of them happened to be in the San Francisco Bay Area at the same time, they decided to get together. The trio met for lunch at a place called Scott's Seafood Grill, of course.

"When we told the hostess why we chose her restaurant, she gave us each a bottle of Scott's Chardonnay," said Wayne Scott from Loveland, Colorado.

One of the Wayne's sent me a brief write-up of the unusual meeting as it appeared in a local newspaper. The headline writer gave it a blasé heading, something along the lines of "Three Scotts Meet at Scott's Seafood."

I thought he missed a once-in-a-year chance to have some real fun. I would have used the headline: "Wayne, Wayne, Go Away."

And that brings us to today and why my work carries the name David L. Price. I feel a need to explain why, mostly because it's not my favorite sobriquet since it seems a bit pompous or elitist, which I hope I'm not.

In a perfect world, I'd just go by David Price. But here's the problem. There already are two somewhat famous David Price's in the U.S. The first is a congressman from North Carolina, where I used to take my kids for summer beach vacations. It's fun near election season to see posters all over the state proclaiming my name. But it's confusing, too.

To make matters worse, with the first pick in the 2007 professional baseball draft, the Tampa Bay Rays chose David

Price, a flame-throwing lefty pitcher who played college ball for Vanderbilt University. Tampa Bay traded him to the Detroit Tigers in 2014.

I admit it's fun to see a Sports section headline that reads, "Price Throws No-hitter." Or a crawl on the TV screen saying, "Price strikes out 10 in shutout win."

I did pitch and play left field up through junior high school and had a long career playing men's slow-pitch softball in a competitive league in Virginia as an adult. But I never had a screaming fastball that could whiff the best batters in the American League, so I realize I'm never going to compete for headlines with the lefty DP.

I considered D. L. Price for a while, but there's already an S. I. Price who writes for Sports Illustrated.

You see the dilemma. I also thought about D. Lewis Price, but it sounds like a children's fantasy writer. And people will call me Lewis and I won't respond.

So it's David L. Price. A Welsh name. Up front. There it is.

So consider this is a plea to parents everywhere, especially ones of child-bearing age. Please stop giving your kids the same old boring names. No more Liam, Ethan or Lucas. Stop using Emma, Olivia or Sofia. Do your kids a favor and give them colorful, one-of-a-kind names like Arugula, Sassafras or Barefoot Bob for boys. Maybe Virgule, Sunflower or Dulcinea for girls.

And if your last name is Price? For the love of Godfrey, please don't call your baby David.

Note: *Part of my daily morning routine involves reading the Police Blotter section of the San Jose Mercury News. Yes, I am among the two dozen people who still get a newspaper because I like the sports section, the advice column, some of the comics and the blotter, which is a sampling of the crimes committed in the cities along the peninsula of Silicon Valley. And it keeps me in a far better humor to skip most of the news.*

One unofficial conclusion I've reached from this regular reading is the inordinate number of crimes committed by people under the influence of drugs or alcohol. Does this mean we're trying to stop crime only through punishment? Maybe we could squeeze from the budget a few more dollars for treatment, rehabilitation and prevention? Just a thought. Written in fall 2013.

Crime in the City

You can learn a lot about the darker side of humanity by reading a John Steinbeck novel or listening to an opera by Mozart. You can also witness the nasty underbelly of how some humans act under pressure by imitating Jane Goodall and watching adult fans at their young kids' sporting events.

"There's no way in hell my little Xenophobia was offside!" screamed a tall, bird-like man in pale yellow Bermuda shorts last weekend at the girls' U10 soccer game I watched. The veins in his neck threatened to explode and splatter deoxygenated blood over the dark blue-and-white striped golf umbrella that half-matched his navy polo shirt.

176

Sorry, pal, but any poor girl you named "Xenophobia" is bound to have trouble with strangers in her life.

Yes, these are all good examples of the shadowy side of Homo sapiens. For me, though, I prefer digging even deeper, learning all I need to know about the human condition – as seen through the eyes of Hieronymus Bosch – by regularly reading the Police Blotter in the Local section of the San Jose Mercury News.

The Police Blotter is ominously subtitled: "Crime News from Selected Cities" and the blurbs that follow recap the reasons our police officers are sent into the streets to stop the miscreants who have gone Cro-Magnon on their fellow civilians. The reported incidents cover a wide array of crimes, including shootings, stabbings, road rage, thefts and other unpleasant and terrifying human interactions.

One of the first important conclusions I came to after a few weeks of avid Police Blotter reading, is that about 95 percent of the criminal acts in our communities are committed by men and women who are, shall we say, at least a few sheets to the wind. The car thieves, assault committers, road ragers and other criminals almost always tend to be higher than Ben Franklin's kite on crystal methamphetamine, marijuana, alcohol or some combination of the three.

And now that methamphetamine has climbed so much in popularity that it's referred to as the toothless man's cocaine, criminals are typically apprehended when they are wired to the gills and as hyperactive as a pack of Irish wolfhounds raging on 60 mg. of Prednisone and running at you as if you had roast chicken smeared across your belly.

Fortunately for us, amid the daily blotter's litany of aggression, misery and legal troubles, lays the occasional nugget that is so outlandish and special it not only makes us wonder about the future of the species, it also makes us laugh. Here's an example from Santa Clara:

3700 block of El Camino Real, 10:43 p.m., Thursday. A man swinging a machete to defend himself against the imaginary snakes inside his parked vehicle was arrested. According to police, the man was extremely intoxicated from glue sniffing.

Items such as the one above raise all kinds of questions, including: How did the model plane turn out? What happened to the snakes? Did they take them to the zoo?

At least the fellow was parked. Can you imagine seeing that car weaving in and out of the lanes next to you while you're driving down the highway and heading home from work?

This next one is my personal favorite, involving one of the oddest – or at least slowest – examples of road rage ever. It's from the city of Burlingame:

1100 block of Trousdale Drive, 4:57 p.m., Tuesday. A disturbance involving two wheelchair users who backed into each other while boarding an elevator was settled.

It's hard enough to be confined to a wheelchair without getting whiplashed from behind. But trying to roll and fight simultaneously requires a special type of skill, according to my friend Michael, who has been a wheelchair wanderer for decades.

You can test yourself the next time you're in a crowded produce market early Saturday morning at the start of a three-day holiday weekend and the better part of the city's great unwashed are pushing their shopping carts aimlessly through the narrow aisles without the slightest notion of how much space they're taking up and refusing to yield after several polite attempts to get past. If that makes you want to ram the holy hell out of someone, you should start preparing for your own immortalization in the Police Blotter.

Here's a recent item that shows how alcohol can make even the most mundane acts seem suddenly hilarious:

1500 block of More Avenue, 10:23 p.m., Wednesday. A male who lit a friend's shirt on fire with deodorant spray had his friend's permission.

Sure, go ahead and spray me with Axe. Then light me on fire and we'll see what happens.

I simply can't imagine something like this happening to sober individuals. This kind of idea only makes sense when your blood alcohol content looks like a decent batting average. My guess is that the Internet went down while they were watching the world's funniest hits to the male groin area on YouTube and they were forced to find another way to amuse themselves.

And here's one from Atherton, my favorite city in the Bay Area. Atherton is where the very wealthy commune with each other and the police are always at their beck and call:

Greenoaks Drive, 7:53 p.m., Monday. A resident worried that a noisy hawk in a tree was in some sort of distress. When authorities arrived, the hawk was quiet and enjoying dinner.

That's the most excitement they've had on Greenoaks street since 10 years ago when a brazen 17-year-old youth had the audacity to raise the flag on a resident's mailbox when — get this — there was nothing in it!

But none of the other listings can compare to this one from Redwood City, a decidedly lower-income area than Atherton:

Hoover Street, 10:14 p.m., Thursday. Police say six pairs of shoes were stolen from a second-story balcony.

This should be the easiest crime to solve in the history of Redwood City policing. I mean, just how many very tall, 12-footed burglars are out there in the Bay Area?

And if it's true crime doesn't pay, the best example I can think of is coming home with six pairs of used shoes. If I worked for the Redwood City police, the first place I'd check is the bowling alleys.

Note: *Have you ever panicked when one of your cats or dogs is missing after you move into a new place where the territory, landmarks and scents are completely different? I certainly have. I clickety-clacked this column in March 2007.*

My Kitty Companion

Spencer the Wonder Cat – my boon companion, kitty poet and pillow mate – took off the other day. It happened right after we moved into my like-new mobile home, the last affordable housing in Silicon Valley.

It was so hot that day you'd brand the back of your thighs if you leaned bare-legged against something metal. So I opened the doors to try to conjure a cross breeze and the rascal bolted.

I found him next door on the west side, sitting in a sun spot, doing advanced calculus problems in his head or whatever it is cats do when they lounge in those rays that have come so far just to warm us.

I slipped my fingers under his front paws and pulled him away from his calculations. He gave a protest meow – not an angry one, but an indication that, for the record, he had been quite close to solving a difficult problem and would now have to start over.

I took him back inside and shut the doors. Spencer is an indoor kitty. After years of having cats with outdoor privileges and paying hundreds and hundreds of dollars in veterinarian bills to patch them up after nocturnal bouts of feline fisticuffs,

I decided to limit Spencer's world to the 867 square feet of my previous two-bedroom apartment.

Now that we've relocated into a relatively spacious 1,100 square feet in our very own double-wide, I chose to make Spencer a kept cat and an inside one at that.

Somewhere in the continuing chaos of moving in, he slipped out a second time. It was, after all, unbearably hot and I guess I left the door open again as I fluttered about, unpacking boxes and attempting to instill some order onto this colorful collection of clutter.

I called for him and there was no answer.

"Spencer!" I yelled.

Nothing.

So I searched the Lilliputian backyards of my new neighbors, adding the sound of his name to the casual chittering of all the birds and squirrels.

"Spencer!"

No answer.

Also for the record, my catastrophic thinking can go from zero to 120 faster than an Italian teenager in his daddy's "borrowed" Ferrari. Spencer had been gone for maybe 10 minutes and my mind had him without anesthesia on a cold metal table in an unscrupulous perfume-tester's laboratory, strapped down and yowling for help.

I walked up and down my curving street with all the homes side-by-side. If I were up in a helicopter, the homes would have looked like members of a marching band spelling out the "S" in Spencer in a football stadium.

No answer. So I took several deep breaths, thought about the mental tools at my disposal for calming myself and — here's a concept — actually used them.

I did the half-smile, a great trick I learned in a mindfulness class. With this technique, you relax the corners of your mouth into a neutral position, then slightly pull them up into a smile, mimicking the famous one on the Mona Lisa's face. You do the same thing with your eyes, pulling your entire face into a half-smile.

I know it sounds silly, but it is an incredibly powerful meditation technique. The other day, a Yahooligan cut me off while driving and then compounded his transgression by flipping me off. As I felt testosterone contracting my body into a massive fist of retribution, I remembered to half-smile.

The simple act of breathing deeply and half-smiling stopped my anger cold. It was as if the gods had dropped a prize-winning Halloween pumpkin onto my internal surge protector, immediately shutting off the power to my Y chromosomes. I continued driving — calm and at peace — and completely ignored the miscreant.

Although the half-smile allowed me to regain my perspective, it didn't bring Spencer back. I went inside, planning to try again at dusk.

My mind rolled tapes of Spencer in my head as I waited for darkness to fall. My kids and I had rescued him from our local Humane Society when he was a three-month-old ball of fur. I picked him because he's a handsome cat with his charcoal-grey-and-black markings, his blazing green eyes, those black tiger stripes across his grey-and-white face, the classic tabby "M" on his forehead in black with white highlights, and the tuft of snow on his chin.

He looked healthy and energetic, scampering through his cage. Little Spencer purred when I held him, resting his tiny head on my arm. We were sold.

After filling out several forms and swiping about a hundred and fifty dollars onto my credit card, my "free" kitten came home with me.

And now he was three years old and gone. At dusk, I walked up and down the mobile home park, in between the doublewides, calling his name. I even walked over to the adjoining neighborhood on the other side of the park, where modest houses cozy up to our trailer park, like lovers lying spent front to back.

Nothing. So I said my prayers and went to bed, fully expecting him to make his way back home by morning, even though he was unfamiliar with the new neighborhood. I left my windows open so I could hear his pitiful cries when he came back, demanding food and a soft bed to lie on.

Morning came. I walked outside. I strolled over to my neighbor's backyard. No Spencer.

My 13-year-old daughter, Ellery, had spent the night and she was upset, too. So she set to work on my PC making a flyer we could pass around. She downloaded a picture of our missing cat, importing it into my word-processing program. I added the title, "Missing!" along with Spencer's description and how to contact me.

Ellery helped me go door-to-door, which is way outside my comfort zone. But I screwed my courage to the sticking place, as Lady Macbeth would have liked, and searched for my errant knight of the dinner bowl.

We passed out more than 70 flyers, leaving them on the doors of each mobile home. If someone seemed home, I knocked on the door and explained our search. All seemed friendly. Some had stories of their own lost pets to share. Some didn't speak English as a first language so I pantomimed Spencer's escape and my search.

They pantomimed back some form of "No, I haven't seen him," or "Go away, crazy gringo!" Either way, I thanked them and we left.

We returned to my home hot, tired and discouraged. I drove my daughter over to her mom's house, ran a quick errand and went back to my place. Once inside, the gods told me to launch another search party. The feeling was vague but powerful and I believe it's rude not to answer when the universe calls.

It was about noon, 24 hours after Spencer took off, when I walked outside. I went next door first and thought I saw something grey 50 feet away, sitting on its haunches in the backyard near a small pile of rotting wood. I walked toward the animal but it scurried away.

Spencer? Is it Spencer? But he wouldn't run from me. We were boon companions, snooze partners, cat-brush compadres.

I caught up to the animal, which was trying to burrow into the wood pile. I saw the end of its black-and-grey body and yelled Spencer's name. I bent down to try to scoop up the furry mass in case it was Spencer and as I touched the animal, it yowled loudly and twisted away.

It was Spencer!

"You crazy cat!" I shouted. "What are you doing?"

I cradled him with both arms, which seemed to bother him less, but he still tried to pull away.

I carried Spencer inside and examined him. He was hot, very hot, and he swore in salty cat language whenever I touched his side. He was hurt. My immediate guess was that he had run into the neighborhood trailer-trash bully, a savage, tattooed, buffed-out, Big Gulp-glugging beast who attacked my Spencer, a bookish, refined, civilized, NPR-listening cat who's in touch with his feminine side. Spencer never had a chance.

So I found a local 24-hour, seven-days-a-week veterinarian clinic online and drove Spencer over. An interminable wait later, a doctor examined him. I pointed to a small tuft of fur stuck together on his right side. She pulled it off, revealing a puncture wound through his grey skin.

One ironic thing about cats is that they have the healing powers of a super creature. If they get a cut on their body, it will close very quickly, almost before your eyes.

However – as with all super creatures – this preternatural healing ability comes at a cost. If a cat is bitten through the skin, its wound will close off within a matter of hours, leaving the bacteria from the other animal's bite inside with no place to go. The bacteria procreate as all God's creatures are wont to do and the result can be a nasty, potentially fatal, abscess.

The doctor caught Spencer's wound before it could completely close over, which meant he was probably bitten in the early hours that same day. So after shaving off the fur around the puncture wound, giving Spencer an IV-bag of fluids, and treating him with antibiotic and anti-inflammatory shots, my kitty was saved – for a total of $225, including the weeks' worth of pills I needed to give him twice a day.

It seemed a bargain compared to past emergency vet bills. So I swiped it onto my faithful credit card and thanked the staff.

As I drove poor Spencer to the safety of home and recovery, my thoughts turned to my wonderful friend Vivien. She's an ebullient, smart and lovely Chinese colleague in her early twenties who not long ago came to the San Francisco Bay Area to work for a month. She chose Vivien as her English name.

Vivien lives in Shenzhen, China, and worked in employee communications at one of my previous company's hard-disk-drive manufacturing plants. She reported to me on a dotted-line basis and came to San Jose to learn about our American culture and teach us about hers.

Vivien taught me a great deal about how employee communications works in her country and the existing cultural barriers. I reciprocated, explaining what did and didn't work among U.S. high-tech workers.

During one of our many lively chats, I told her about Spencer and mentioned that cats had recently overtaken dogs as the most popular pet in the U.S.

"Do you have a pet?" I asked her.

"Oh, no," she answered, shaking her head and frowning.

"Why not?" I pursued.

"In China, we're still trying to feed ourselves," she said, with no hint of irony or malice. It was a simple fact, a truth with a small "t."

"We're not ready to feed an animal, too," she continued.

It made sense. I suddenly felt silly and embarrassed. We have so many riches in this country compared to almost everywhere else in the world. And we extend this wealth and our love to cats, dogs, horses, birds, lizards, snakes, amphibians, fish and other animals.

We're a country in the enviable position of being able to care about the welfare of a turtle when there are so many human beings in the world who go to bed hungry every night.

So one day, as the Chinese people use their entrepreneurial skills, hard work and access to western markets to get wealthier and the Communist state falls — its back broken by the weight of 1.3 billion people yearning for blue jeans, YouTube and freedom — maybe then my friend Vivien will get a larger salary and adopt herself a cat.

This will give Spencer a kitty pen pal in China. And Vivien and I will make a pact that stretches across the Pacific Ocean. To protect our extended family members — and to keep them from squandering their precious lives — both of us will do our best to keep our dear kitties inside.

Note: *Here is the tale of my short professional radio career and why I'm no longer working in the field. It's one of the sad humiliations in my early life that alternate with these happy little stories. I wrote this in 2013.*

Nerve Wrecked

I must have been standing behind the sousaphone player the day God handed out musical ability. My pitch is far from perfect and I can't play a driving, New Orleans-style, boogie-woogie riff on the keyboards – even though I wish I could.

I can play guitar a little, but can't finger-pick the strings and notes so it sounds like icy-pure water rushing over the rocks of a Colorado stream, though I'd love to do so.

Truth is, I can barely play a jukebox. But God compensated by giving me a pretty baritone voice.

Many, many years ago, I parlayed my pretty voice and my adoration for music of all kinds into an evening radio show on my progressive college radio station, which is probably trebly redundant. Wednesday night from 6:00 to 10:00 p.m. was mine, and my voice and my favorite songs shimmered through the cool night air of San Diego, on a good night reaching oh, maybe 20 listeners.

After I left college (finally graduating on the three-college, five-and-a-half-year, liberal-arts plan) and returned to my home town of Englewood, Colorado, I landed a professional radio gig at an easy-listening station on the far western edge of Denver. It was so far out of town and so isolated that no one dared spin "Play Misty for Me."

The hours were horrendous: 10:00 p.m. to 6:00 a.m. on Tuesday, Wednesday and Thursday night, then 6:00 a.m. to 4:00 p.m. on Saturday and Sunday. With the constant ping-ponging between night and day shifts, I don't think I got a decent night's sleep the whole time I worked there.

While on the air, every 15 minutes I would say some variation of "All music, all the time. KLIR-FM." Every hour, on the hour, I would prepare and give a three-minute newscast, ripped and read from the Associated Press wire service ticker in the back room.

The job itself was OK, but I was in my early twenties and eager to learn. And there was never anyone there to teach me anything because they had all gone home and left me there alone. So I endured six months of this and then quit to look for a better radio job.

I found one as a news reporter for Denver's most popular country station, KLZ-AM. My biggest responsibility was delivering hourly news reports on the air, pulling stories together from two wire service tickers. I would re-write the stories from the wire services – mostly the transitions – so the five-minute newscasts flowed smoothly.

One of the more interesting aspects of the job was the placement of the on-air news booth. It was a tiny, glass-walled room with the country station's much larger on-air deejay room to the left at a 45-degree angle. The company also owned an FM rock station and its on-air booth angled off to the right at the same angle.

When I reported the news, the Freudians among us would say I was the ego, with the superego country station to my left and the id of FM rock to my right.

Certain benefits accrued from having the FM station next door. One of the deejays was an attractive, well-built blonde woman in her early 20s. She had an occasional habit of waiting until I started reading the news – totally engrossed in my job – and then pounding on the heavy double-glass window separating us, which listeners couldn't hear because of the directional microphone.

When I turned to see what was going on, she pulled her navy-blue T-shirt up to her neck, baring her lovely, bring-a-friend breasts, which she then proceeded to press up against the glass.

Yes, I stumbled in my newscast that night. Radio listeners have no idea what goes on in the background sometimes.

All was going relatively well with the new job, except that I was getting more and more tired. In addition to my 20-hour a week radio gig, I also worked a full-time day job as a correspondent for a mutual funds company. It was perhaps the worst professional writing assignment you could have: For eight hours a day, I wrote dull, humorless letters to people who were trying to cash in their mutual funds because the policyholder, usually the husband, had died or because they had some kind of question or complaint.

Since I worked my correspondent job during the week and my radio job on Friday, Saturday and Sunday, I never had a day off. This continued for 76 straight days – I kept track as some screwy badge of honor. And ever since I came down with my first outbreak of Crohn's Disease when I was 14, whenever I became physically or emotionally exhausted, my mouth would break out with a handful of nasty, aching aphthous ulcerations, more commonly called canker sores.

Near the end of my streak without a day off, I had an excruciating outbreak of the terrible things, including a large open sore on the side of my tongue – the worst possible place for a radio announcer. It hurt every time I talked and especially when forming any sound that put my tongue in contact with my teeth.

I was at the station one Friday night in this exhausted state. After pulling together the hourly newscast, I went into the on-air booth to deliver it. I looked to the left for signs of activity from the country deejay. Then I glanced to the right, always on the lookout for a wayward breast or two.

The clock on the wall above the control board continued its climb to the top of the hour. Now there were 5, 4, 3, seconds to go. I clicked on the microphone and...

Nothing came out. No pretty voice; no self-assured newscast; no nothing.

I hit the cough switch that all radio stations have. It immediately silences your microphone so the listeners are never forced to listen to you cough or sneeze. I cleared my throat. And I was shaking.

I stumbled through the newscast as if I'd never spoken into a microphone before. When I started back in college, I was nervous in the beginning, as most everyone is. But I had long since conquered the fear of speaking into a microphone with the public listening and had always been able to make the butterflies in my stomach do barrel rolls and loop-de-loops – until now.

When I finished, the country deejay called over.

"You all right?" he asked.

"Fine, thanks," I lied. "Just had something caught in my throat."

It was the final newscast of the evening, thank goodness, so the audience was smaller than it normally is. But tens of thousands of people tuned in to the station – tens of thousands of people. Oh, my God. I hadn't really thought about that before.

It seemed as if overnight I developed the worst case of canker sores I'd ever had, along with the worst possible case of stage fright. The idea of going on air on Saturday made my throat tighten and my stomach churn.

So I tried to relax in a socially acceptable way. Before my next shift at the radio station, I poured three fingers of my father's Jack Daniels (I was living back at home temporarily for the first time in four years because I was broke) into a highball glass. I swirled the amber-colored liquid to let it mix with air before pouring it down my throat in four long glugs. I remember it burning its way down as it passed over the holes in the tender tissue of my mouth and esophagus.

When I got to work, the news reporter going off the air came over to say hello.

"Whew," he said, waving his hand back and forth in front of my face, "you smell like a distillery."

That comment alone was enough to start the panic rising up from inside me.

"The alcohol didn't work!" I shouted to myself. "There's no way I can go on the air. I can't do this, I'll screw up!"

Since avoidance of humiliation is the real mother of invention, I divined what seemed like a brilliant solution. I would gather news from the two wire service feeds and write the news as quickly as possible. Normally, it took about 50 minutes, but I vowed to get it done in 40.

Then I'd slip into the on-air booth, which had a bank of cassette recorders for playing news clips, and record the next hour's five-minute newscast onto a cassette.

Neither of the deejays would think anything of this since they were busy with their own shows and it was routine for the news reporter to come into the on-air booth to work on stories or record voice-overs.

The rest of my plan called for me to walk into the booth a couple of minutes before the hour. I would sit in the chair as I always did and ease the cassette I recorded earlier into one of the players. When the second hand of the clock stretched to reach the top of the hour, I would press the play button on the machine. And as my pretty voice played from the cassette, I would lip-synch the newscast, mouthing the words as if I were doing it live.

It worked great and no one suspected anything as I shuddered with relief. Sure, I'd have to work harder than ever from now on, but I had a solution to my stage fright.

So every hour on the hour for the next week, I lip-synched every single newscast on KLZ-AM with no one suspecting I was faking it.

Meanwhile, my canker sore explosion grew faster than a rabbit colony near the runoff of a Viagra factory. The additional stress, the physical exhaustion and the unabated use of alcohol as an anti-anxiety medication combined to crush my immune system. My canker sore count had increased into the low 30s – an all-time high – in various shapes and sizes inside my mouth and upper throat.

Later in life I would realize the outbreaks of canker sores were an early-warning system indicating the beginning of an eruption of Crohn's Disease, which is an auto-immune-system disorder where your T-cells mistakenly attack the healthy tissue in your digestive system, causing inflammation and painful ulcerations throughout.

I also didn't discover until then that alcohol aggravated the illness. Drinking Jack Daniels when stressed was like tossing gallon jugs of napalm into a campfire to put it out.

I drank Black Jack before every news shift to "relax," then I swished and swallowed mouthfuls of Chloraseptic anesthetizing mouthwash to temporarily kill the pain in my mouth and throat before recording each newscast.

My desperate plan to keep my job worked fine for a week. But early Saturday evening, a large apartment complex caught fire and we had a man on the scene to give a live report. I would have to talk to him on the air to introduce what was happening and there was no conceivable way I could record it ahead of time although I wasted valuable minutes trying to think of a way to do so.

I ended up recording everything but the introduction of the man on the scene. As the top of the hour inexorably approached, I tried as hard as I could to calm myself. I filled my head with thoughts of the color blue. I took deep breaths to quiet my thoughts through self-hypnosis. I even hummed a cheerful version of "Twinkle, Twinkle Little Star."

195

But as I walked into the on-air booth like a condemned man climbing the stairs to his hanging, my heart beat like a set of tympani in a walk-in closet. I sat in the chair and watched the second hand move menacingly toward the top of the hour. I hit the switch that put me on the air, pushed the cassette button and heard my pretty voice say, "You're listening to KLZ-AM in Denver. It's 8:00 and here is the news."

Then I hit the microphone switch and stammered through the lead-in to the main news story and the introduction of our man at the scene. I'm hoping to this day that I didn't do as badly as my memory tells me I did. All I know is that I was shaking when I finished lip-synching the rest of the news.

I stumbled out of the booth and over to the telephone. I dialed the number of a friend who also worked at the station as an on-air news reporter, a fellow who got the job because of my recommendation.

He was home, thank goodness, and could come in to relieve me, but he didn't have a car. So I left the station and drove to his house, which was 15 minutes away. I sped through the Denver night with all the stories for the next hour's news. He pulled them together into a newscast in the passenger seat as we headed back to the station.

My friend went on the air at 9:00 as if nothing had happened. After he finished, I asked my friend to call the news director and tell him that I had to quit. The director asked to speak to me but I shook my head, "No." I was too humiliated and upset to talk to him directly. I was 25 years old and my radio career was over.

Numerous surveys have shown that the number one fear everybody has is speaking in front of a group of people, more than twice their fear of dying. That means the ultimate fear must be giving your own eulogy.

From that day on, whenever I had to speak in front of a group – even in a small business meeting – I suffered a horrendous case of the jitters. I finally figured out what was driving this fear: An ugly voice in my head telling me over and over that I was a fraud, that I was a failure. The voice, which first whispered its way into my life at the radio station, made me doubt myself and question my abilities, despite any evidence to the contrary.

Years later, I now recognize that ugly voice as the alcoholic and addict inside of me. It had been unleashed by the combination of genetics, physical exhaustion, a chronic illness and my progressive reliance on alcohol to change the way I felt about myself. For decades, the voice wanted to make me so fearful, so uncomfortable in my own skin, that I would drink or use drugs to numb myself, change the way I felt and try to silence those awful noises in my head.

I finally stopped relying on drinking and self-medication in August 2005. Thanks to the advent of new biologic medications – currently delivered with a biweekly shot that I give myself in my belly – my Crohn's Disease is in remission and I haven't had a canker sore in years.

It took regular practice, prayer and years of therapy for me to overcome my stage fright by learning to believe in myself, live in the moment and have an honest understanding of both my strengths and my limitations. I've received a lot of practice speaking in public through regular sharing in Alcoholics Anonymous meetings and I simply don't get nervous in front of an audience anymore. I rarely hear that ugly voice these days and when I do I've learned techniques to make it go away.

I'm clean and sober now, thanks to the grace of a loving God – the same one who passed me by when distributing musical ability – and the unconditional support of my friends both inside and outside the program, as well as my family, too.

I realize it's probably way too late in my life to resume a radio career. But if I ever do, one of the most important requirements hasn't left me.

I still have a pretty voice.

Note: *The genesis of my prescription-drug addiction is chronicled in this story, which has not been published until now. Also described is the beginning of what AA folks call "my bottom." It began the evening I realized my addiction was stronger than my love for my children – a truly frightening moment.*

Captain Hooked

In the summer of 1999, I was chewing on a hard pretzel when one of my favorite molars snapped off below the gum line. I barely avoided swallowing the enamel-covered hunk of calcium and spit it into my hand. Then I called my local tooth practitioner, Dr. Jollymour, who sounds like the dentist in a Dickens' book.

He cleaned up what he could and sent me to a periodontal surgeon, who performed brutal, medieval procedures on the tender tissues of my mouth. Without going into stomach-turning detail, let's just say that he cut into and removed a chunk of my gum so he could build up enough of a base to eventually place a crown on the remaining part of the tooth.

Anytime you leave a dental professional's office with your legs trembling and an enormous bag of ice pressed to the side of your face, you know you're in for a painful night or three. It explains why I also left with a prescription for 10 days' worth of Vicodin – something I'd never taken before.

I filled the prescription at my local pharmacy, returned home and popped two of the long, white pills with the rounded edges into my mouth. I swallowed a huge gulp of water and continued to take one every four hours or so over the next three days.

As a long-time sufferer from Crohn's Disease, there are at least two things that every afflicted person has in common: continued bouts of pain in your lower abdomen as your biologically confused T-cells attack the healthy tissue of your colon – where my disease shows up – and frequent diarrhea as a result of the ulcerations this creates.

After three days of Vicodin, I had neither. The pain in my gut had completely subsided and – if you wanted to – you could have bronzed my firm, award-winning poops and displayed them at the Museum of Modern Art.

For the first time since I came down with this chronic illness at 14 tender years of age, I was thrilled with my overall health. So I made an appointment with my gastroenterologist, who I enjoyed and greatly respected. He is now retired.

My doctor explained to me the many benefits of opiates, the class of drugs Vicodin belongs to. Each Vicodin tablet is composed of hydrocodone – an opiate – and Tylenol, a brand name for acetaminophen. A regular Vicodin tablet contains 5 mg. of hydrocodone and 500 mg. of Tylenol, which is the equivalent of one extra-strength pill.

Opiates have been around since the Chinese took turns smoking it from the communal hookah instead of mowing the lawn or washing the rickshaw like they were supposed to be doing. One of the more modern commercial forms of opiates used at the turn of the 20th Century was laudanum, a bitter-tasting, reddish-brown liquid. The directions call for you to put a few drops under your tongue or into a glass of water and drink it. Within moments, the world becomes hazy and heavy and all your cares melt into the floor beneath you. Laudanum was prescribed for various aches and pains, and was a popular palliative for what was once called "women's troubles."

According to government statistics I discovered online once, the number three cause of death at the beginning of the 1900s was diarrhea. I know it's an unpleasant thought, but can you imagine shitting yourself to death? What a way to go, so to speak.

But there it was, squeezed behind cancer and heart disease. I'm sure they lumped together all kinds of intestinal disorders, ranging from influenza and food poisoning to the less common intestinal bowel diseases such as Crohn's and ulcerative colitis. Besides, doctors weren't as anal, if you will, about causes of death as they are now.

My doctor said he could prescribe laudanum for me so I could receive the same bowel-soothing effect of someone in Doc Holliday's time. He assured me, however, that I wouldn't much care for it.

So he happily wrote out a scrip for Vicodin instead, four to six tablets a day, with three refills. I filled it immediately, popped two in my mouth, chased them down with a glug of water and lit the long, slow-burning fuse that didn't explode for about seven years.

Maybe two years into my habit, I suffered a severe attack of Crohn's so we increased the dosage. Before he started to get wise to my addictive ways, we had progressed to Vicodin

HP tablets, which contained 10 mg. of hydrocodone and only 325 mg. of Tylenol.

In my addiction-addled mind, I thought I was doing my body a favor by doubling the opiate and dropping the amount of acetaminophen. A similar line of thinking is this: If your hands are cold, you can warm them immediately by sticking them into the flames of a lit burner on your gas range.

Unfortunately, that's how we think. We want something and we want it RIGHT NOW! It's how we're wired. I'm convinced I was born an alcoholic and drug addict. It just took some time for the behavioral side of things to catch up with the genetic one.

For years, the first Vicodin or Vicodin HP tablets in the morning gave me a feeling of warmth, coupled with a slight euphoria. It was as if I were seated in a heated, lightly vibrating chair with my senses perfectly balanced between relaxed and highly alert. I would pop the pills in the morning, get ready for work, walk to my car, fire it up, hit "Play" on my CD player and escape into a private cocoon of my favorite music.

The tunes sounded and felt so unbelievably pure and sweet. The music swirled through me and carried me away to a paradise where all my needs were met and all my troubles had been jettisoned in a heap at the station. Jimi Hendrix described it completely with two words: Purple Haze.

Unfortunately, that phase of my opiate use didn't last very long. My unofficial anecdotal research shows that Vicodin tends to have a completely different effect on addicts than it does on "normies," the term we use to indicate the 90 percent of the population who aren't wired like we are. Many of the opiate addicts I've talked to say something similar: When normies take a Vicodin, it either gives them an aching stomach or makes them feel as if they're walking underwater while lugging a crate of bowling balls. Vicodin makes addicts speedy.

So it all seemed perfect: a readily available, affordable drug that killed my pain, worked as a constipating agent and filled me with energy! Alas, as every parent in the world has said to every child since the world began: Cutting corners may get you there faster, but at what cost?

For much of the time I took Vicodin, I also was taking Prednisone, the manic child of wonder drugs. The combination made me feel nervous, impatient and aggressive while also making me act grandiose, entitled and invincible. Sure, it enabled me to work 50+ frenzied hours a week, including nights and weekends.

I was so fried by the time I got home that I had zero tolerance for my wife, who is a lovely, intelligent, very talented woman. She is wired to process information slowly, thoroughly and in-depth while I'm as impulsive as a diva on amphetamines — ready, fire, aim is good enough for me.

In my executive communications work at Hewlett-Packard, the company was in the midst of a raging dispute over the acquisition of Compaq Computer and a battle for the very soul of the once-proud company. The pace moved like the roadrunner after a double espresso — beep beep.

Most of our attempts at communication between my wife and me would devolve into a verbal paintball battle and I would either take sniper shots from the doorway or just escape to the bedroom where I didn't have to engage in such niceties as talking to people.

She kept her thoughts and her anger to herself and it took her several days to get over being annoyed with me, if she ever got over it at all. As I sank deeper into my Vicodin and Prednisone addictions, I masked months and even years of exhaustion and regularly expressed my frustrations with her. This made her continually angry under the surface, but nothing was ever said.

Based on my experience, what they say about the genders and sex is completely true. A man needs to have sex to feel close and a woman needs to feel close to have sex. My constant anger pushed her away and our lack of a fulfilling sex life made me frustrated and even more angry. This was not a recipe for a happy marriage.

Meanwhile, I kept ordering my Vicodin HP, now through a mail order pharmacy. Every three months, a package arrived at our front door with a massive white plastic pill container inside. Each one contained 540 tablets and I was as happy as a kid at Christmas to hold that container in my hands.

More than six years of this later, it began to occur to me that I might have a problem. My wife rarely spoke to me. Our marriage was no fun at all. We tried joint counseling but gave it up when we realized how angry we both were and how wide the gulf between us.

One week, I finally confessed my continuous drug use to the therapist I had started to see and she was appalled. It was the only thing I had ever lied about to her.

That's when I decided to try to at least control the amount of drugs I took. I had been a maintenance user for years now. Every day I took two tablets before leaving for work, two just before lunch, two in the late afternoon and two when I got back home in the evening. Eight extra-strength tablets a day was my habit, the equivalent of 16 Vicodin daily.

As an experiment, I decided to stop taking the two pills at night. My ritual was to come home, drop my briefcase, hug and hold my children, take off my shoes, and walk over to the kitchen cabinet that held my pills. This time, when I stood in front of the cabinet, I focused on a mental image of the things I loved the most in my life – and that was our twins, who were 10 years old at the time and I just adored them. I told myself that if I loved my children as much as I know I do, I would walk away without taking those two more pills. I stood before the cabinet, some days as long as several minutes, burning the image of my little ones into my conscious mind. "Don't do it!" I said to myself. "Don't do it!"

And every time – every single time – I would sigh, open the cabinet door, shake out another pair of tablets and swallow them with water. My addiction was stronger than my love for my children. I realized it then and it frightened me to death.

At some level, I had consciously painted myself into a corner. I had ratted myself out to my therapist, who was now after me weekly to quit my habit. One session she even told me that she would drop me if I didn't do something about my addiction. Here's another clue you might be an addict: Your therapist threatens to drop you because of your refusal to quit.

I told my wife, who has some serious codependency in her genes. Even she questioned whether I had a problem.

Since there are no coincidences, about that time a newsletter arrived from the Palo Alto Medical Foundation, where my doctors practice. On the back page under the Health Bulletin section, I spotted a listing for a weekly two-hour session with a doctor who specialized in alcoholism and addiction with the come-on: "Do you have someone in your life who might have a problem with drugs or alcohol?"

Yes, I certainly did. It was me.

I attended the next session, where I was the only practicing addict/alcoholic, all the others were the spouses or parents of someone with the problem. Also attending was a man named Barry Rosen, may he forever rest in peace. Barry was the managing director of a substance-abuse treatment facility in Redwood City, California.

During the meeting, I briefly shared my story. Barry came up afterwards and told me he could get me off the Vicodin any time I was ready. He gave me his card.

I went home that night and mentally calculated how much Vicodin I had taken over the past seven years or so. With two years of popping Vicodin tablets and almost five years of taking Vicodin HP – plus the extras I managed to score when I ran out early and played three doctors against each other to get more – I had swallowed more than 23,000 Vicodin tablets, a truly frightening amount. That's while also taking the equivalent of more than 16,000 extra-strength Tylenol, by the way. Or 160 of the 100-tablet bottles.

How my liver managed to function through all that is astounding and one doctor told me that, at the end, every pill I took was like playing Russian roulette with that uber-forgiving organ.

I woke up the next morning exhausted and ready to declare defeat. My plan was to call Barry's recovery center and my medical insurance as soon as they opened to see if my plan covered rehab. Before placing the calls, I opened up the cabinet, focused on the image of my children, sighed like air rushing out of a blown tire and took two more Vicodin HP. I knew it was time to surrender.

Note: *Right after I hit my addict/alcoholic bottom in early 2005, I was checked in to the lovely beige-walled Psychiatric Ward of Stanford Hospital. I'd already been through rehab, but it was a tumultuous time in my marriage and I simply broke down right after the Ides of March. The ward seemed like the safest place to go. For the record, I have changed the name of my roommate.*

Angel Eyes

I arrived at the Stanford Hospital Emergency Room on the night I hit bottom and spent the next few hours drinking a vile-tasting liquid potion with more vitamin B-12 in it than you'd find in a standard National Football League training room. After I'd taken my last stomach-churning sip, I was moved by gurney to the Psych Ward where every door carries my favorite sign: "Caution – danger of elopement."

I wasn't sure if it meant I'd get the honeymoon suite or if they just had a high ratio of hook-ups among us loonies inside. It took me about four days before I thought it was funny. It simply means: Don't let the psych inmates out.

Taking barbiturates ordered on the Internet, drinking vodka and thinking about ending my life was as low as my journey went. And unlike Hollywood movies where you roll and sweat for a few days and then things immediately get better, I bounced along the bottom for months, like a water skier who falls but refuses to let go of the rope and is dragged flailing behind the boat.

Three days after I checked in, they moved me out of the first room they'd assigned me, which was one step above the classic padded-wall room. It was Asian in its simplicity with the single bed neatly made and on the floor. It also was practical in its lack of anything sharp or dangling.

I had a roommate this time. Andy was a quiet, almost timid man in his mid-50s. He had trouble sleeping so he was often awake at night after lights-out. One evening while most of the other patients slept, we chatted softly about our lives as we lay on our single beds. He told me the story of his father, who shocked Andy's family by killing himself with a rifle shot through his head when Andy was 12 years old and beginning to struggle through adolescence.

He talked about how sad he was that he never got to know his father as an adult, that the man never taught Andy how to drive or drink or handle himself in the world. And he wondered how much pain his dad must have been in to do such a terrible thing as end his life. Then Andy started to cry quietly, with the tears running down his lined face and into his bushy gray moustache.

I watched him cry and was horrified at what would have happened to my dear children if I had gone further than just think about ending it all. They were completely innocent and I almost made them casualties of my mental illness. Until that moment, I never realized what a terrible thing I'd thought about doing.

I knew then that my Higher Power, whom I choose to call God, had sent me another angel. I see them from time to time and every angel I've stumbled upon has either pointed me in the right direction or taught me a lesson I desperately needed to learn.

The first time I bumped into an angel came when I was 21 years old. I had saved enough money to take a trip to Manhattan from my home in Englewood, Colorado. My much older second cousin, Ken, was a well-respected vice president in the publishing business and my naïve self thought I could fly to New York, get a few introductions from Ken and land a job writing in the center of the literary world. Easy, right?

The first night, I stayed at Ken's house and made the mistake of trying to keep up with his drinking – cocktails before dinner, bottles of wine with dinner, whisky afterwards, then the cognac. I got stinking, staggering, room-spinning drunk and spent the better part of the night head down in the toilet, violently throwing up.

Somewhere during the night, I remember Ken standing at the open door of the bathroom after I'd loudly thrown up and stage-whispering down to his wife, "He's got his mother's stomach."

When I struggled down for breakfast the next morning, Ken's wife – who was almost blind due to a tumor on her pituitary gland – said, "You're not the first one he's done that to."

Meanwhile, Ken was cheerful and energetic the next morning, as if alcohol never had any lingering effect on him whatsoever. Years later, as his wife's health declined and Ken felt increasingly sorry for himself, he drank himself to death. The disease of alcoholism runs deep in my family, especially on my mother's side, although it skipped both my parents.

During my New York trip, Ken did introduce me to some powerful people, but they were too high up in their organizations to really help me. And I was there the week before Easter, so many of the high-level managers I talked to were eager to wrap up and hit the road for spring vacation.

This was my first real-world introduction into the publishing business and I started to realize it was not going to be as easy as my callow, 21-year-old mind had thought.

Four days into the trip I began to panic. I only had a couple of days left and no one had come close to offering me a job. Ken had a meeting that morning so he dropped me off at a cavernous bookstore in midtown Manhattan and told me he'd pick me up in about an hour.

I walked back and forth through the rows of books, getting more and more anxious. I started pacing the aisles furiously, sweating in the on-sale, light-gray, three-piece suit covering my skinny young body.

I almost jogged to the back of the store where I found an old wooden staircase that led to the upper reaches of the three stories of books. I climbed the wide stairs up onto the second floor, which seemed smaller than the first. There were books everywhere, mostly filed neatly in row after row, but some piled on the floor.

A smaller staircase led to a closed door above. This stairway was narrow, darkly lit and had an off-limits, employees-only feel to it. But there was no sign. So I marched up the dozen or so steps, swung open the door and barged inside.

An older man, maybe on the northern side of 60, was sitting quietly maybe 20 feet away, near the end of the triangular room filled with books of all kinds and sizes. His long, salt-and-pepper beard tilted toward salt, especially where it twisted down into the book he was reading. The man had this halo of brown and white hair around his head and his fingers were thick and hardened, as if from a lifetime of manual labor.

His marvelous eyes told me he had seen just about everything in his time on earth and he was neither soft nor cynical because of it. Stacks of books rose around him toward the dirty skylight far above.

He took in the sight before him, this sweating, anxious young man, looking for something, anything, but not really knowing what.

Our eyes met and he held his stare for what seemed like a thousand years. Then the man spoke.

"Patience," he said, with a voice that seemed like a two-note blurt from a bassoon. He turned back to the thick, ancient book he was reading. And apparently the conversation was over. It seemed as if I'd only deposited enough money for a one-word answer to my many pressing questions of life. More experience, more trauma, then healing – that'll be $10, please.

I bowed slightly, which seemed like the appropriate gesture, took two steps backward and left his room. I shut the door quickly and closed my eyes to fix the scene upon my memory. Who was this man? Why was he up in this room? Why had he said what he did?

Looking back at this more than 30 years later, I know full well what he was. He was an angel – nothing more, nothing less. He was there to teach me an important lesson: That nothing worth doing comes easily; that you need to work hard and steadily toward your goals and never give up when misfortunes come your way or others doubt. You need to trust your inner voice – the one that speaks to you in those quiet, meditative moments – and ignore the negative self-talk of the addict within, the smooth-talking Mephistopheles that wants you to succumb to the disease.

Of course, you need to balance your belief in yourself against the cold, detached test of reality. If your goal passes this test, move forward with hope, faith and passion.

As I get older, I watch for angels more carefully and listen to them more closely. They have always been there for me and have yet to steer me wrong.

Back in the hospital room that night, I watched Andy cry. Forty-three years after his father took his own life, his son still grieved as if it had happened yesterday. The wound in his psyche never completely healed.

I felt awful watching him cry. I hugged my children in my head, realizing what I had come too close to doing. And my tears began to fall, too.

Two broken men lay in that room, each trying to find a way to stop the pain or at least keep it at arm's length for a while. At that moment, crying together was the answer.

I'm still working on patience.

Note: One thing in this world truly disgusts me and sits on top of my personal all-time gross-out list: throwing up. In my view, that's the only acceptable word to refer to the act, with the possible exception of vomiting. This is the topic for this little tale, along with an example of how bone-headedly many men play with their little boys and the strange metamorphosis most humans go through when they become parents. It's truly amazing what you can instantly overcome when you're in charge, there's no time to ask and it involves your child. This one stars my wonderful son, Owen, and was written about a decade ago.

Members Only

If you're a woman and you read every one of the following 854 words, your reward will be this: You will learn everything you'll ever need to know about men. Imagine that – in only 854 words. (You're not counting them, are you?)

And if you're a man? Consider this a warning.

When my son, Owen, was just shy of two-and-a-half years old, we lived in a rented house in Menlo Park, California. One day, I was lying on the couch when he toddled over. As background, Owen was one of the happiest kids I've ever known. He was curious, bright-eyed and had this wonderful habit of jumping up and down and dancing with glee every time I came home from work.

He is now a teenager. Enough said.

Back then, when he was in his third year, he toddled over to me, I picked him up and then lay back down on the

214

couch. I lifted Owen above me with my arms extended so he was parallel to me, his face directly above mine. And I started jostling him, shaking him from side to side, like a can of new paint in a shaker. Every time I moved him, he giggled and giggled.

I bent my arms and brought Owen down so we were nose-to-nose and then pushed him back up. And I jostled him some more. This, of course, is how guys play with their children, whether they're boys or girls.

The physical play made us both laugh out loud, with Owen making that infectious little-kid giggle that is one of the world's sweetest sounds.

So I brought him down one more time and quickly pushed him up as high as I could. As I wiggled him, he stopped giggling and his whole body seemed to shudder. He had this odd look on this face, like he was pondering something deeply. So I stopped shaking him but still held him at arm's length above me.

He seemed to take in a shallow breath and then he vomited, full force, straight down into my face. My son, his cheerful self transformed instantly into the Duke of Hurl.

Now, it's important to point out that I have always been squeamish about people throwing up. I hate to watch someone do it in person or in a movie and always close my eyes. I hate the sound of it. I hate the smell. I even hate the slang words used to describe it. And here I was with a face full of vomit – my glasses completely covered – running down my neck and into my shirt.

In between the spasms, Owen started wailing. I brought him down close to me and held him to my chest as I slid off the couch, holding him tight. I felt my way toward the bathroom around the corner since I couldn't see through my glasses, which were ground zero in the attack. I stumbled once but didn't come close to dropping him.

When we reached the bathroom, I put him down and started stripping off his clothes and then mine, as he continued to cry. I removed my glasses, took off my shirt and turned on the shower above the bathtub. As the water began to pour down and bounce off the porcelain surface of the tub, Owen shrieked, "I don't wanna take a bath!"

I tried to comfort him but to no avail. He was standing there naked with his eyes closed and dripping tears. I yanked off my pants and then underwear, holding him with one hand, while feeling for the temperature of the shower with the other.

"I don't wanna take a bath!" Owen screamed. "I don't wanna take a bath!"

When the water was warm enough, I picked him up and placed him standing in the tub as the shower rained down. I climbed in after him, holding on to his shoulder for support. Owen was closer to the shower with his back to it and I stood in front of him.

He let out one more protest of "I don't wanna take a bath!" and then opened his eyes, which were now clean and free from any signs of vomit. He looked straight ahead at my naked body and became completely calm. And with an emotionless, little-boy voice he said:

"You have a penis, too?"

At that moment, the crisis dripped into the tub along with the vomit, swirled around the drain and disappeared into the pipes.

Yes, my son, I have a penis, too. You don't have the only one in the world, although it may seem that way to you and to every other male. Learn to master the urges of your penis, my son – instead of letting them master you – and you will lead a full, rewarding life.

And one other reminder? After you use your penis to relieve nature's call, please do yourself a favor and learn to put the toilet seat down. It's a small gesture, but one that will go a long way toward making the females in your life happy – and that's a darn useful thing to remember.

Note: Ah, yes, the one percent really do lead such very different lives. It's certainly true in my part of the world and we call one of the towns they inhabit Atherton.

Only in Atherton

It's not just sour grapes when I say that the one percent live very different lives than the rest of us. Through exhaustive research while lying on my bed, I have discovered incontrovertible evidence to prove my point, thanks to the San Jose Mercury News and the Police Blotter in the Local section.

The Blotter is a highly entertaining feature that logs the crimes committed in the local cities comprising the breadth of Silicon Valley, from San Jose in the south to Foster City or San Mateo in the north. When you peruse its daily listings, you'll see crimes like this one, which happened in San Jose:

3200 block of Impala Drive, 6:57 p.m. Monday. A 17-year-old is expected to survive after being shot in the back by someone who fired at the group of males he was standing with. According to police, the shooting was gang-related.

Here is another typical entry, which happened in Santa Clara, just north of San Jose:

Washington and Newhall Streets, 10:34 p.m. Wednesday. A driver was arrested for speeding, driving under the influence and possession of methamphetamine. According to police, the driver also had a large sum of cash and paperwork indicating drug sales.

Crimes such as the two above are commonplace in the cities of Silicon Valley. But every few weeks the Blotter would include very different listings from a city called Atherton, which is just north of Palo Alto. Let me share a quick story to explain what Atherton is like.

When I planned to move my family to the San Francisco Bay Area from Arlington, Virginia – just a mortar shot across the Potomac River from the nation's capital – I first visited the Santa Clara County Sheriff's Office. One of the tips I've picked up when moving is to visit a local police station and find out where the majority of the crimes are committed so, if you can afford it, you can stay away from those areas in your hunt for a safe place for your family to live.

At the office, a uniformed man with thick forearms and a pleasant smile pulled out a large map that showed the number and types of crimes committed per zip code. It was easy to see that the bulk of the shootings, stabbings and drug crimes occurred in a few particular areas in San Jose. Also clearly evident was one particular zip code where almost no crime took place: 94207.

While looking at the map, I put my finger on that section.

"That's where I'd like to live," I told the man.

"So would all of us," he said with a laugh. "That's Atherton. It's where the rich people live – former NFL players, owners of businesses, heirs to fortunes."

I had explained to him that I was looking to rent initially and would like at least a two-bedroom home with two bathrooms since my wife and I had young twins just over a year old.

"No offense," he said, "but I don't think Atherton is for you."

We settled into a much more affordable part of the Bay Area and this was my first indication that Atherton is a very different part of town. When I started my regular reading of the Police Blotter, I learned just how different.

Here is one of the first Blotter entries for Atherton that I saw, featuring an incident that happened several months ago:

Irving Avenue, 7:47 a.m. A landlord/tenant dispute involving "assault with frozen food" was reported.

I could picture it immediately: A 50-year-old white male snapped and went after his 60-year-old white male landlord because his freezer wasn't cold enough. First he tossed a melting cherry Popsicle at the landlord. Then he grabbed a stack of moist Lean Cuisine butternut squash ravioli and threw them one at a time, Frisbee-like, at the man. After that, the guy went completely nuclear and fired the remaining contents of the freezer at the landlord, including ice trays, while screaming, "They're melting. They're melting!"

I was hooked after that. I eagerly awaited each edition of the Mercury News to see if this were typical for Atherton or just a one-time aberration. Surely, I thought, Atherton must have its share of violent crime, like this listing from San Jose:

600 block of Nordale Avenue, 8:11 p.m. Tuesday. A 15-year-old boy was struck in the head with a cinder block by several men during a gang-related attack. His injuries were not life-threatening.

I was happy to see that the young boy survived the horrible crime. But after I read it, I noticed the bold subhead "Atherton" lurking in the next column of type. I immediately shifted my focus to the listing, which said:

Coghlan Lane, 7:33 p.m. Friday. A woman told police someone was at her door and that when she asked who it was, no one answered. Police responded and determined the stranger outside had delivered a package.

I'm so relieved to learn that the Atherton police spend their valuable time solving such mysteries. Those of us who tend to isolate from the world can well understand how awfully intimidating that darn doorbell can be. ("Oh, God, there's someone there. Call the cops!")

As the clippings piled up, they seemed to indicate that the population of Atherton – the very rich, the one percent – tends to be on the conservative side and perhaps a bit further along the aging continuum than other parts of the Bay Area. I also concluded that – although violent crime rarely if ever happens to these people – they are still a bit jumpy with all that property, fine furnishings, fancy cars and electronic toys to protect.

I've also found that it doesn't take much to annoy the denizens of Atherton, based on this Police Blotter listing from the day before Christmas last year:

100 block of Reservoir Road, 10:47 p.m. Dec. 24. Police responding to reports of a suspicious person hollering "ho-ho-ho," encountered a male in a Santa costume who makes a habit of going up and down the street greeting his neighbors every year.

And as the police drove him away, he proclaimed in a voice loud enough to disturb his neighbors, "Merry Christmas to all, and to all a good night!"

So there you have it – proof positive that the people in Atherton live very different lives than the rest of us. And even though they remain unsullied by violent crime, they are always on high alert for any kind of interruption to their pristine peace. Here's a listing to confirm it:

200 block of Oak Grove Avenue, 3:04 p.m. A male was reported to be lying on the ground, possibly writing.

That was me, by the way. And Atherton must be the only place on God's green earth where something like that could be considered a crime.

Note: *I've had a love/hate relationship with engineers all my life, beginning with my father, who was a mechanical engineer. Most of the engineers I've worked with seem to think in a different way than I do and many also seem to disregard the work writers do. There are some wonderful exceptions to this observation and these engineers have become dear, life-long friends.*

This article stems from my early days at a Hewlett-Packard sales office and the way some of the management sales people (who were all engineers, too) seemed to unconsciously denigrate what I offered the team. Then this phenomenon spread to Palo Alto when I moved west to continue with company.

Verbiage

Most of my professional work has been done in the famous, innovative and extremely self-important Silicon Valley – the area in California south of San Francisco and north of Morgan Hill. Only 40 years ago, the area was thick with lush orchards growing plums, prunes, cherries and other kinds of fruit.

Today, it's corporations, start-ups, shopping malls, houses, apartments and strips of small businesses lining El Camino Real from San Jose to San Francisco. It's still beautiful, but one can only imagine with a stinging sense of sadness how stunning it once was.

If you live in Silicon Valley, you know that you can't throw an iPhone 6 without hitting an engineer – which sometimes seems like a good idea. Just kidding, engineers!

I've worked with lots of engineers in my career and mostly adore them. They can do all the things I can't from installing more memory in your PC or fixing a broken washing machine to designing and installing a spectacular Christmas light display that's synchronized with classical music and broadcast for blocks on an unused AM radio frequency. They can even program your sprinkler system without staring blankly at the instructions for hours at a time like I do. Engineers are darn useful people and I know this.

I've also worked with many sales and marketing people who are blessed with their own impressive skills. They typically smell terrific, dress nicely, have lovely smiles and regularly display the tenacity of a Gila monster whose jaws are clenched around your forearm and squeezing at the rate of 1,500 pounds per square inch. (The engineers will have to tell you how to measure that.)

The successful sales and marketing people also drive fancier cars than I ever will and have an ability to talk strangers into just about anything and make them feel good about themselves while doing so.

But here's the rub, as Hamlet might say. Most of the engineers and sales people I've worked with have little-to-no appreciation for the skill and effort that goes into stringing words together effectively. They think everybody learns how to write in elementary school and the smart and capable ones have moved on to something more useful.

Although I'm reluctant to generalize quite so broadly, they seem to be as sensitive to the needs of us emotionally driven writer types as a scorpion is to its morning meal. Here's an example that makes the top number of my blood pressure read like a decent bowling score.

In my professional experience, whenever engineers or sales executives refer to the beauty of words carefully crafted, those pearls of prose pieced together with the skill and precision of a master jeweler, they always — without fail — use the word "verbiage."

Oh, you've heard them do it. They sit there in the meeting rooms and say it with a dismissive flick of their wrist, as if writing were the essence of insignificance, lower in the scheme of things than a dung beetle's bottom, as disposable as a square of toilet paper stuck to the sole of their imported Italian shoes.

"And then," they say, "you can add the verbiage."

It's the way they say it. It's as if — in their minds — "verbiage" is a cross between "vermin" and "garbage." And not just any vermin and garbage. It's a bloated, bubonic-plague-infested Norwegian wharf rat with pus oozing from its open sores and a dump-truck load of putrid, steaming, maggot-wriggling trash that's been coagulating for a month in the sweltering heat of the sultry summer sun in Washington, D.C. That's what they seem to be saying.

Well, at least that's what it sounds like to me, he sighed.

So whenever anyone dares to say "verbiage" in front of me during a meeting, I fine them a dollar and give them the long explanation why. Sometimes they laugh. Sometimes they just stare.

I'd be living in a palace in Barbados by now if they simply would have paid me.

Note: *At times I've managed small teams of wonderfully talented and self-driven communications professionals and I had one cardinal rule (other than all the little language guidelines I imposed): While we can go so far as to use "position" to describe what we do in employee communications, we will never use the word "spin." In other words, we always need to tell employees the truth, with a small "t."*

Unfortunately, in spring 2002 I was given a conflicting mandate and push came to shove.

With a Small "t"

For the better part of my professional career, I've worked in employee communications for high-tech companies like Hewlett-Packard, Hitachi Global Storage Technologies and then Gilead Sciences, an incredible biopharmaceutical company that has contributed enormously to making HIV/AIDS simply a treatable disease rather than a death sentence. These companies are so complex and rapidly changing that it takes people like me to help employees understand what in the world is going on and where the company is heading.

What's most important about employee communications is trying to help employees connect the dots from the company's business goals all the way back to their individual jobs. This helps them decide if their daily priorities are relevant and lets them see that what they're doing on a daily basis is important, that they're part of something that matters – something bigger than themselves.

One of the job's responsibilities is to write the chief executive officer's internal messages. This includes the company vision, quarterly results explanations, progress updates, slides, webcast talking points, video or podcast scripts, and all those organizational change memos that arrive in your electronic In Tray.

At HP, I wrote for chief executive officers Lew Platt and Carly Fiorina. When friends from other companies and other disciplines asked me what I did, I often told them I was the Memo Writer to the Stars.

In a job like mine, if you earn the trust of the CEO, you can have incredible access to the top decision-makers. And if the company truly believes in open and honest communication (I can count them on my toes), you can even tell the truth most of the time (with a small, humble "t," of course). You never get to tell the complete, 24-karat kind of truth for obvious reasons – highest on the list is to avoid panicking the masses and the shareowners in hard times. At a place like Hewlett-Packard, there was a time when you could come very close indeed to telling the God's honest truth.

In fact, one day at HP, I did tell the unvarnished, raw-as-a-newborn-baby's-butt truth. By the end of the next day, I was gone – figuratively at first, then, oh so literally. It turned out to be the personal wake-up call I needed and my subconscious mind, as always, was a couple of strides ahead of my rational, day-to-day brain.

In any job – depending on your personal values, your financial circumstances and your market value – you need to be willing to walk away if you're asked to cross an ethical line. That's what happened to me.

The best advice I've ever heard on the topic comes from Chuck House, a former HP leader who spent 30 years with the company before leaving to work with software start-ups. In a Fast Company article in the late 1990s, Chuck was asked the rhetorical question: Can you tell the truth without jeopardizing your career?

"My honest answer is, you never know until you try," Chuck said. "Three decades ago, as a naïve young engineer at HP, I persisted in championing an idea despite opposition. I came away from the whole experience with a motto: Come to work each day willing to be fired."

I whole-heartedly agree. You can only spend so much of your life standing on the bank watching the river flow by. Sometimes you have to close your eyes and jump in. And see where it takes you.

In my opinion, even on your worst day in the profession, employee communications is a far more honest place to work than the marketing department, which is where some companies relegate us. In marketing, the skills required are similar, the pay is better and everyone dresses a lot nicer.

But you have to be good at something I'm terrible at, which is – to be kind – always spinning the apple so only the good side shows. You never let anyone see the bruises or the discolorations when you're in marketing. In good employee communications, you have faith in the overall intelligence of your audience and the strength of the company to show them the entire apple – with a rational explanation of how the soft spots got there, what the company is doing about them, and practical tips and guidance on how the individual employee can help.

When I led a team – both at HP and then later at Hitachi – I banned the folks who reported to me from ever using the word "spin."

"We can go so far as to say 'position,'" I told them, "but I never want to hear 'spin' – because it implies that we're lying and that's something I refuse to do."

Here's a story about the difference between strong employee communications and marketing. In April 2000, Carly Fiorina, then CEO for HP, and her marketing minions had an actual replica built of the garage where Bill Hewlett and Dave Packard started the company in 1938. They paid tens of thousands of dollars to build this ersatz garage on a grassy knoll on the grounds of the company's Hanover Street headquarters in Palo Alto, California.

This is where they shot the commercials the company ran that year – you may have seen them – with Carly in her Armani suit, leaning against the garage and purring with that sexy voice of hers – the one that sounds like a Siamese cat after a lung-rattling hit of good Mexican pot.

On the same day the advertising agency had dozens of people scurrying around to shoot these commercials with Carly, a modest home stood on a quiet residential street about a mile away. At 367 Addison Avenue in Palo Alto, the real garage still stands, the place where Bill Hewlett and Dave Packard began perhaps the greatest adventure in technology and enlightened management in history.

In 1989, to celebrate the company's 50th Anniversary of incorporation, an aging Bill Hewlett was driven to the original home of HP and dozens of employees had gathered to celebrate with music and an ice-cream social.

As a car crept up Addison Avenue, Bill looked out the rear window and asked the people with him, "Which one is it?"

While everyone paid all this fuss to honor the company's icon – the garage – its co-founder had never been back and was never interested in going back. The only icons he cared about were hard work, creativity, treating your people with respect and beating the competition.

Although Bill and Dave never cared about the garage, Carly resurrected it and, while CEO, continually spun the founders' legacy and mythology to suit her purposes. It may have been good marketing; it was lousy employee communications. And, in a truly karmic sense, it eventually came back to bite Carly in her well-dressed behind when the HP Board of Directors fired her in February 2005.

Back in early 2002, I had a moment with Carly that told me all I needed to know about what was becoming of the once-and-future Hewlett-Packard. We were in a meeting with the head of the communications department and a handful of other people. The topic was how to rally the HP masses so they would support Carly's plan to acquire Compaq Computers – something the founders' children were furious about.

I began to speak about the importance of maintaining our credibility with the employees. We need to be upfront with them, put out accurate information and get them on our side by treating them like the intelligent adults they are.

Carly interrupted my little speech.

"Whenever there's a revolution, the army takes over the television stations," she said. "David, you own the television stations," Carly continued, referring to my management responsibility for the team that produced the Newsgrams that went to all employees in the company; our intranet site, hp.Now; and the "Apparently So" blog I wrote every couple of weeks. In the blog, I tried to speak the truth with a small "t" in every online edition.

"You control what people see and read," Carly said. "Manipulate them!"

"Manipulate them?" I thought to myself in horror. I tried to keep a poker face because I found myself instantly in dangerous territory, miles behind enemy lines. I disagreed to my very core. That was the polar opposite of what I believed my role to be, the antithesis of effective employee communications.

She meant that she wanted me to spin the information we provided, to show only the bright and shiny side of the apple.

I smiled wanly and said "So you want me to come over to the dark side, huh?"

Everybody laughed. But that was the moment Carly lost me.

That was the moment I knew my long HP career was over.

A few months later, the company offered an early retirement plan to employees who had at least 15 years of service and were at least 50 years old. I had worked at HP for the required 15 years – starting in Gaithersburg, Maryland, and relocating to corporate headquarters in Palo Alto, California – and I qualified for the age requirement by 19 days.

I was the first of my dear friends in the communications department to leap from the mother ship, free fall through space and yank on the rip-cord of my parachute, which was anything but golden.

It made me ponder for a long time what you need to do to succeed as a company. At its essence the formula is simple:

1. Provide something of value.
2. Hire good, self-motivated people.
3. Give them something meaningful to do.
4. Make it easy for them to own at least a small piece of the company.
5. Tell them the truth about the health of the business.
6. Let them decide what needs to be improved at their level.
7. Get their input on how to do it.
8. Let them lead the effort to fix what needs fixing.
9. Show them how their progress is contributing to improving the company.
10. Celebrate when they reach a milestone.

Rinse. Repeat. And whatever you do, always tell employees the truth, at least with a small "t." Because once you lose their trust, it's over and no amount of spin will ever bring them back.

Note: I realize that my mind can make some unusual leaps and bounds. Here is a column from Tieline East in the summer of 1989 that proves the point. It bounces from a celebration of the moon landing in July 1969 to a part-real, part-imagined history of the Druids and Romans, along with waxing poetic about that lovely orb sailing through the night sky about 239,000 miles away from us. It all makes perfect sense to me. How about you?

Howlin' at the Moon

Twenty years ago this summer two human-type critters took an earth-lit stroll across the dusty surface of the moon. Neil Armstrong and Buzz Aldrin bounced around for two hours like a couple of little kids in designer snowsuits. Then they headed back to terra firma, leaving behind assorted junk including the lunar landing module, a couple of golf balls and some Tastykake wrappers.

Landing on the moon and returning unscathed was a great moment in the history of human pursuits. The adventure demonstrated the loftier side of the human beast: We can accomplish some amazing feats when we focus our collective talents on achieving a unified goal.

Meanwhile, the neighborhood dogs on Earth howled at the ripe Florida grapefruit above, just as they always have. They didn't much care if some scientists from Houston had drawn a moustache on the man in the moon.

For umpty-ump thousands of years our mystic moon has cast its spell on creatures of the night, the better of whom include poets, lovers, magicians and wolves. Oh, and Druids, of course.

The Druids were my ancestors, a splinter group of Celtic types who hung their horned hats in Wales and parts of Ireland and Scotland. Wizards, not warriors, led the Druids, an intriguing people who shared an abiding love of nature and an equally powerful distrust of any authority other than their own. Many years later, they would become coal miners, Dylan Thomas and King Arthur, of all people.

The Druids had a weakness for the moon, especially when it flooded the midnight sky, full and bright, floating like a radiant ovum on a sea of India ink. A moon like that wreaks havoc on the creatures below. It's the kind of moon that drives your cats to play jai alai with your underwear at three o'clock in the morning. And it's best for all concerned if you're not in them at the time.

The effect of the moon on the Druids was equally dramatic. When the glorious orb slipped over the top of the trees and into the midnight sky, my ancestors held secret pagan rituals. At the height of their passion, they painted themselves blue, climbed trees and howled at the moon – a practice still observed by the odd member of Congress.

Unfortunately for the Druids, their historical timing was off. During the heyday of the Druids, the Romans had grown bored after slicing France into *tres partes* and headed north to the British Isles looking for fresh territory for Julius Caesar to write about.

A couple of millennia ago, the Romans were the Donald Trumps of the world, acquiring everything in sight and putting in nice plumbing.

One night, after a hard day of building aqueducts in Wales, some Romans snoozed by the fire dreaming of Domino's pizza when piercing human screams split the night air. The soldiers leaped out of their goose-down sleeping bags, grabbed their spears and ran toward the sound.

After fighting through the brambles, they came upon a clearing and saw something that gave them pause, if not fast forward: a dozen blue, human-like creatures hanging upside down and naked in the trees, howling at the moon.

The sight scared the olive oil out of the Romans. So they reacted the same way all conquering people do when confronted with something they don't understand: They slaughtered every Druid they could find.

For some reason, the Druids upset the Romans like no other group of humans. Nobody else could hold a candle to them as far as the Romans were concerned.

It's a shame, too. If the Romans had been less hysterical about it, they might have picked up a few useful tidbits from my nature-loving, moon-worshipping ancestors. Not even the most sophisticated, technologically advanced culture on earth has a corner on all the wisdom in the universe. Besides, if the Romans and Druids had become cozy, think how much easier if would have been for a certain someone to pass high-school Latin.

We've done some astounding things in the past few decades. We've advanced our technology with laser strokes of brilliance, making lasting leaps of progress in many fields.

Yet improvements in human understanding have come at a glacier's pace. Despite our marvelous inventions, there are still plenty of Romans in the world, still a lot of Druids.

Twenty years ago this summer, a man took his first tentative steps across the dusty surface of the moon. It's the same moon my ancestors howled at thousands of years ago. It's the same moon I'm going to howl at tonight. Arrooooooooo.

Note: *In spring 2013, I spent most of my time writing freelance feature articles for the employee intranet of Gilead Sciences in Foster City, California. This meant I logged plenty of hours burning fossil fuels while driving back and forth on Highway 101. The good news is that I finally bought a new car in December 2013 and doubled my miles per gallon, up to about 41 or 42. Just trying to save some money and do my part along the way.*

Running on Empty

It was right there at the tippity-top of my To-do List: Fill the car with gas. But I didn't awaken early enough before heading to work in the morning. When I'd accomplished enough tasks during the day to avoid teetering into the self-inflicted hell of missed deadlines, my subconscious carjacked my motor skills and I drove straight to the comfort of home instead of taking the longer route to the gas station.

Sure, I could have gone out last night after I finished my evening chores, which include feeding my two felines and making sure the older one eats from the bowl on the right with the wet cat food in it instead of gently pushing his younger brother out of the way and poaching from the bowl of wet adult cat fare on the left. (They have become so accustomed to my meal-time corrections they automatically switch back to the proper bowl when they hear me coming, as easily and effortlessly as a pair of yellowtail fusiliers gliding in an underwater school near the Marshall Islands.)

Unfortunately, it was well past dark by then. I was as weary of the world as Portia in "The Merchant of Venice" and as tired as a two-month-old baby who's finally stopped crying after her first DPT shot.

I weighed the choices in my head. Option A was to pull on my navy hoodie and comfortable shoes, drive over to the local gas station, slip my debit card into the slot, get bombarded by the shrill commercials screaming at me from the pumping station's TV monitor and clean my car windows with the worn, wobbling squeegee that a thousand other people have already coughed, hacked upon and grabbed with their bare, flu-ridden hands.

Or there was Option B: Ease into the brushed-cotton comfort of my cozy bed, feel the cats cuddle up to my reclining body as my breathing slows and I slip immediately into the replenishing arms of sleep.

I'll get gas in the morning, I told myself.

An hour or so after the first rays of dawn, a short burst of sports talk radio awakened me. I tried to tug my still-unconscious mind away from its delectable dreams while the cats swam in shark circles across the bed with their tails straight up like dorsal fins. After just another five minutes, please, I rolled out of my nightly womb to face another day.

Soon the tea kettle whistled the news that the temperature of the roiling water inside had reached 212 degrees F., or 100 degrees C. for my friends outside the U.S.

I transferred the water into a pot holding black tea from India, quietly ate breakfast and then did my best to make myself presentable enough for human contact.

Since it was getting near time to leave for my first meeting, I started scrambling like a bride getting dressed for her wedding. I brushed my hair, stuffed my notebook and laptop into my computer bag, clipped my entry badge to my belt, poured some Tejava iced tea with a jolt of lemon into an insulated travel cup and headed for the door.

I started my car and the first thing I noticed was the pale red light of the gas pump icon on the dashboard, just above the fuel-tank indicator. It was the incessant reminder that appears when the amount of gas in the car is starting to get as low as a centipede's ankles.

As the engine awakened, the red arrow on the indicator pierced the top of the letter "E." Since this wasn't the first time I'd run quite low on gas before refilling — have scientists been able to sequence the human procrastination gene yet? — I knew I should have just enough to drive the 42-mile round-trip to work and home again, a bit less than two gallons.

I had the first interview for my freelance job in about 45 minutes and you could never tell whether traffic on Highway 101 from Moffett Field near Sunnyvale to San Mateo in the north was going to be sailing smoothly near the 65 mph speed limit or whether you'd be memorizing the bumper stickers on the car in front of you while crawling along at single digits. Since I didn't have time to stop for gas before work, I slipped my car into gear and joined the horde of other drivers trying to be somewhere else.

I arrived at work on time and went about my day. Around 3:00 I had done enough at the office and decided to head home so I could beat the evening crush hour. My plan was to put in a few more hours of work from my home office, where I split my time.

The red light of the gas pump icon glared at me as I started my car. Although the red arrow now sliced through the bottom half of the "E," I knew there was still some wiggle room. I'd never put more than 15.3 gallons into my tank so I figured the capacity must be 16 (isn't trial and error so much more convenient than actually opening the manufacturer's guide in the glove compartment?). And hadn't the arrow gone all the way below the "E" at least once before? I was supremely confident I had plenty of petrol for the 21-mile ride home.

I zipped down Highway 101 at 72 miles per hour, keeping up with the flow and listening to KQED, our local National Public Radio station. Just more than halfway home, I was captivated by a spirited discussion on who was more to blame in Congress and the White House for the continuing inability to deal with the budget impasse, which had just led to automatic spending cuts of $85 billion in programs neither of the major political parties wanted to cut.

I was shaking my head at the sheer bone-headed insanity of everyone involved when the engine in my trusty Honda CR-V seemed to stutter for a moment. Since I was flying down the highway in the fast lane at the time, it struck me as odd.

I eased my right foot off the gas pedal slightly and then pressed it harder, expecting the engine to roar in response so I could continue breezing down 101 as I passed the Oregon Expressway exit. But instead of surging ahead as it usually did, the engine lurched forward slightly, seemed to hover in space for a moment and then shut down completely.

I had no power at all and was suddenly gliding on momentum instead of internal combustion. The car immediately started to slow down.

So I did what all men do in this kind of emergency: I shut off the radio. We are hunters not gatherers and – because of this fact – can only focus on one thing at a time. Women, by contrast, have been blessed not only with the ability to multitask but the capacity to excel at it while simultaneously carrying on a complex conversation. We members of the XY Tribe don't have the genetic coding for multitasking and you're lucky to get a Cro-Magnon grunt out of us when we're concentrating.

So with the annoyance of the radio silenced and my pulse rate approaching my weight, I flipped on my right turn signal and tried my best to ease over from the far left lane. Between some very nice people and enough natural breaks in traffic, I was able to slide over one lane at a time through the stream of cars as my speed declined.

By the time I reached the slow lane – with my hazard lights steadily flashing – my car felt as heavy as a ceramic rhinoceros. It moved slowly forward, now with enough cars behind me in the slow lane to hold my own Thanksgiving Day Parade. To add music to the procession, a few motorists honked their displeasure at having their precious paths impeded.

What made the situation frighteningly dangerous was that this particular part of the highway has been under construction since Calvin Coolidge ran for office. The section I'd reached had a 42-inch-high concrete Jersey barrier abutting the slow lane, which left no shoulder area whatsoever for me to escape the heavy flow of traffic.

The Honda traveled another 50 feet or so until it slowly, slowly, slowly rolled to a complete stop, blocking the far right lane entirely. I shifted the automatic transmission into park, engaged my emergency brake and picked up my cell phone, which I felt most fortunate to have with me. It even had some charge left.

I thumbed the number in my contact list for AAA. Although I had been a member for decades, this was the first time I'd been in enough trouble to need their roadside assistance. And now I needed it fast.

As I listened to the number ring several times, I could feel my pulse thundering on the sides of my throat and in my temples. Car upon car pulled around me and zoomed by, some of their drivers shooting me evil glares. An automated woman's voice finally spoke into my ear and I heard her say, "Welcome to Triple A."

In my rearview mirror, I saw a dark gray SUV swerve into the next lane over. It roared by me as the driver blasted his horn. The Doppler Effect gave it a drawn-out, mournful sound, making it hard to hear the voice on the phone.

She repeated my options and I was having a hard time concentrating with all the automotive action swirling around me. I pressed the "0" key and hoped for the best. A few moments went by and the pleasant voice of a live female human greeted me.

"Triple A, how can I help you?" she asked.

I explained my situation to the woman, telling her how I was stranded on the highway with cars swarming all around me and in imminent danger.

She seemed to know what she was doing and her soothing voice had a mother-of-all-mothers quality to it. I explained that I was stranded on 101 South, had just passed the Oregon Expressway exit and was maybe a half mile away from San Antonio Road.

The names seemed to puzzle her.

"What state are you in?" she asked.

"Oh, crap," I thought. "I'm about to be crushed into Welsh pudding by a monster semi-trailer truck hauling ass down the highway and I'm talking to a woman in the Philippines!"

Another horn shrieked at me as I muttered my mantra to calm myself: Go Gently Through Life, Go Gently Through Life, Go Gently Through Life. Near a state of panic by now despite the soothing effect of the words, I considered crawling over to the other side of the car, out the window and over the Jersey barrier. Then I'd run as far away as my little Welsh legs could carry me.

I was about to act on the impulse when I looked in my rear view mirror and saw a huge white truck with bright yellow flashing lights creeping forward two cars back. One by one – after waiting for openings – the drivers in my immediate wake stomped on their accelerators and screeched by. The white truck rolled forward slowly until it was right behind me.

While watching this curious vehicle, I had almost forgotten the woman on the phone. She asked if I needed a tow truck. As she did, I heard a heavy door close and saw a figure approaching in my mirror.

"Why don't you hold on?" I said into the phone. "In fact, let me call you back."

By then the figure had reached the side of my car. I took another deep, soothing breath. Was I going to get a ticket for stupidly running out of gas on the highway? Or would this guy be nice enough to give me a ride to a gas station?

I was thinking maybe the two of us could manage to push the car out of danger despite the angry cars sailing by when he walked up beside me. I pressed the button to power down my window and gazed up to see a handsome, brown-skinned young man in a dark teal uniform with short sleeves that had two white halos of stripes circling them. I looked at his nametag and couldn't believe what I saw.

It said, "Jesus."

I swear on a stack of bibliophiles that was his name. In the midst of a terribly frightening situation with danger all around, I was about to be saved by Jesus.

In a brief moment of clarity, I realized his friends and family members probably pronounced it "Hey-Zeus."

Either way, the young man explained he was with the Freeway Service Patrol, something I'd never heard of before. His job is to cruise a certain section of Highway 101 in his tow truck and assist stranded motorists so he can help avoid Gordian Knots of traffic snarls on our busy, busy roads. He also told me he'd be happy to give me a free gallon of gasoline in case that's what caused the problem.

"I can't do it here, though," Jesus said. "It's too dangerous."

Wow, I thought. Too dangerous for Jesus. We'd better get out of there fast.

He instructed me to put the car into neutral and take off the emergency brake so he could push me about a quarter of a mile up the road where there was a break in the Jersey barrier. I did as he said and within a few minutes his huge white tow truck had gently pushed my Honda CR-V to safety.

Once we reached the shoulder, he emptied a gallon of gas into my car from a stout red container. He told me to turn the ignition key and my engine promptly started, roaring its eagerness to get back on the road.

I thanked Jesus profusely and twice offered him a $20 tip, which he refused both times.

"It's against our principles," he said.

I thanked him a third time and eased my car into gear. I spotted a hole in the moving horde of vehicles and stepped on the gas pedal. My car responded as it always had before and smoothly joined the flow. I headed home, eager to tell my friends the story of how I was saved by Jesus.

As I pulled away from my roadside savior and his sparkling white chariot, I swore on all things holy this was the last time I would ever take the chance of running too far on empty. And I rejoiced in knowing that whenever I drive through the Valley of the Shadow of Silicon – for all the days of my life – I shall fear no evil, for I know Jesus will always be near.

Note: Here's something I wrote in summer 2014, three months after my diagnosis of cholangiocarcinoma (see Prologue). My sense of humor returned fairly quickly after my death sentence and it's helped me tremendously.

My goal was to see if I could still ride without training wheels.

The Taste of the Teeming Mass

One of the most useful keys to life is learning how to slide down a Bell curve without getting splinters in your butt. All my life, I typically end up near the bottom left or right side of the curves, which represent the various distributions of our teeming masses.

And the subject area where this Bell curve phenomenon becomes most evident to me – Mr. Teeming Mass – is the one accounting for taste.

Take coffee for example. If you're like the great majority of people, you enjoy starting your day with a hot cup of coffee. Whether you alter your java with a shot of cream or milk or a teaspoon (or three) of sugar, it still boasts that rich flavor, whether it came from Colombia, Brazil, Ethiopia or any of the other places that grow, harvest and ship the beans.

As you sip from your steaming mug of Joe, you appreciate the taste and feel the caffeine molecules forechecking their way through your crowded bloodstream as the mocha mojo clears away the cobwebs and fires you up to meet the day.

For me, however, even a tiny sip of coffee makes me gag and spit it back into the cup. To my peculiar configuration of receptor buds, coffee tastes as if someone boiled the soles of my sneakers in swamp water and added a cup of battery acid. I've even tried it with enough sugar to alter the economy of a Caribbean nation, but it doesn't help.

I was in Milan once, thanks to my former job at a famous computer and printer manufacturer. We were preparing a presentation by our chief executive officer that would be broadcast live in front of our Italian sales office employees to sites around the world. The folks hosting our production crew had set up several espresso machines along with a barista to operate them to keep us working at the feverish clip required to meet our deadlines.

I decided if I were ever to enjoy such high-octane coffee, it would be an authentic version of the potent potion while working in Italy. So, a few hours before the show, I accepted the barista's offer of a tiny cup of the brew resting on a doll-house saucer.

I let the highly caffeinated beverage cool for a few minutes, then screwed my courage to the sticking place and took a hearty sip.

As the molecules of the dark brown espresso swirled across the papillae inside my mouth, the taste buds assigned to recognize anything bitter shuddered at first. Then they screamed in agony as if I'd just swallowed a quart of jet fuel laced with cat hair. My tongue tried to retract itself and roll backwards down my throat like a red carpet in reverse.

I dropped my cup, which fortunately didn't shatter when it hit the floor, and I somehow managed to hold everything inside my mouth while frantically looking for a place to spit. Unlike in the movies, there were no potted plants nearby but I did manage to rescue the cup off the floor, which drew me toward it as powerfully as the sight of an oasis tugs at a man dying of thirst in the Gobi Desert. I fumbled to turn the cup upright and, in front of the entire crew, spat the contents of my mouth into it.

Oh, Soul O' Mio, was I embarrassed!

This taste problem gets even worse with the things I do like. Since I also appreciate a morning or afternoon caffeine buzz, I've gravitated to tea, said to be the most popular beverage in the world, although certainly not in the United States.

To satisfy my caffeine cravings, I shop for small tins of loose tea leaves at a coffee-and-tea chain that began here in Northern California. I became especially enamored of a mixture of black and green teas that the enterprising tea-meisters named "Pumphrey's Blend." For years, I chose a quarter-pound container of Pumphrey's every couple of months from the neatly arrayed tins in the store and it became my favorite morning pick-me-up.

Last month, I walked into a nearby store and my eyes flittered like a butterfly on amphetamines across the various tins with their brown labels shouting out the name of each variety. There was no "Pumphrey's Blend."

I glanced through the rows again to make sure I hadn't overlooked something. I even opened the cupboards below where the workers stored more tins. There wasn't a single "Pumphrey's" anywhere.

I asked the tall, early-20-something woman behind the counter if she had any "Pumphrey's Blend" tea in back.

"What's the name?" she asked.

"Pumphrey's Blend," I repeated.

"Never heard of it," she said.

"How long have you worked here," I asked.

"About two months," she replied.

"Is there anyone else who's been here longer?"

"Sure, there's Celeste," she said, pointing towards a blond young woman with colorful glasses and wearing a similar brown apron.

"She's been here a week longer."

"Would you mind asking if she's heard of Pumphrey's Blend?"

She hadn't.

"Sometimes they change them," the blonde woman said.

So I went home disappointed. In fact, I was so disappointed I went to the company's website and wrote a very polite email expressing my displeasure that my favorite tea had disappeared from the shelves.

The next day, a lovely, professionally written email from a woman in customer service appeared in my Inbox. She verified that Pumphrey's Blend had indeed been discontinued. She said their tea menu has been expanding and the retail stores lack the space to stock them all. So they had to cut some teas from the menu.

She didn't come right out and say it, but logic shouts they cut the ones that weren't selling very well. Which meant I was one of a small but loyal group of tea drinkers who cherished poor Pumphrey's Blend and we were all joylessly holding hands as we slid down the far left side of the tea buyer's Bell curve.

This happens to me more frequently than the phrase "turn your dreams into reality" appears in ad copy. Last week my local produce store stopped carrying the black-cherry yoghurt I like because, as the manager told me, "Nobody buys it."

I told her that I did indeed buy it and promised to continue buying four or five a week. So she reluctantly started stocking black cherry again, but it's teetering on protected status if not outright extinction.

On another affront to my taste, I have to drive almost an hour to an outlet mall to find the type of licorice mix I like – this after unsuccessfully scouring the online menu of every sweet shop for 20 miles around me.

I also adore iced tea, but I like it black and unsweetened. When I'm driving around town or on the road and wanting refreshment, every 11-Babeven or Happy's Quick Stop has iced green tea, sweet tea, lemon tea, mango tea, raspberry tea, papaya tea or countless diet flavors but nothing as simple as black, unsweetened tea.

In this age of specialization, manufacturers are trying to appeal to the more esoteric desires of the teeming masses. Meanwhile, Mr. Teeming Mass and his simple tastes have been chucked out the driver's-side window and are becoming just another clump of decaying roadside debris.

So excuse me for a moment while I rummage through my top bathroom drawer for a pair of tweezers. These splinters in my behind are making it awfully hard to sit.

Note: *This column from "Apparently So" also landed me in trouble. I was "hauled into the woodshed" by the head of IT, an old friend from my days in the Eastern Sales Region. I bumped into Mike a couple of days after the column below posted and he told me how irked he was by it.*

I volunteered to come talk to him for the woodshed session and he chewed me up one side and down the other in a very polite way. I ran a follow-up column a week or so later called "Tales from the Woodshed" that presented the IT side. But I still think the way they introduced all the changes was quite unproductive. Maybe I should have helped them?

Dog Puppet

I haven't weaseled my way into serious trouble for a while and my internal alarms are going off. So let's talk about that thing we're not supposed to talk about: the alleged discussions Hewlett-Packard is having to acquire PricewaterhouseCoopers (no relation).

Let's start by not talking about that silly name of theirs. It's a spell-checking nightmare, a car wreck of words. It looks like a ransom note from e. e. cummings. Or a hip-hop accounting firm.

There used to be a time when I would blame the stupid agency that scraped such a ridiculous solution from the bottom of the idea barrel. I have evolved since then. Now I blame the knuckleheaded committee that approved it.

OK. Now that I've dissed the consulting world, let's move on to the Information Technology reinvention that's going on around here. Everybody knows the concept of that famous half-glass of water: optimists see it as half full, pessimists see it as half empty. Realists see it as just another glass to wash.

Most days I'm a half-full kind of fellow. But I'm running on empty, Jackson. And in the spirit of truth, justice and credibility, I think we owe it to ourselves to tee up the painful side of this reinvention and drive it down the fairway like an angry John Daly.

SYSTEM ADMINISTRATOR WARNING. Your mailbox has exceeded one or more size limits set by your administrator. Delete unnecessary files or your mailbox will be frozen.

Drat. There's an example now. How many of you have been subjected to this supreme annoyance over the past few months? Nothing quite adds to your personal productivity like an anonymous, threatening message.

Good corporate citizen that I am, I followed the web link at the bottom of the message. I would have preferred to talk to a human being, but our local IT help desk is now in Bangalore, India, and we're only supposed to call them for system emergencies or to warn them about approaching cyclones.

The link directed me to a web page that offered tips for moving my email folders to my personal hard drive rather than storing them on the shared drives. Somehow this is supposed to save money, but I personally can't understand why storage is cheaper on my laptop than on an enterprise storage device.

I guess the IT folks are so busy trying to save money that they forgot the number one rule of change management: If you're going to take something away from people or change the way they have to work, tell them why. Put it into business context and guess what? Most people are pretty decent and will help you out.

So I spent a half hour that I didn't have to spare trying to understand the densely worded web directions and moving files hither and yon. But I'll suck it up and work a little later today. I'm on board with helping the company reduce its infrastructure costs and invest the money it saves into additional sales coverage so we can continue to grow and profit. No problem. Half full.

I even offered to share the tips I'd learned with my colleagues in our department since they had all been randomly erupting with creative combinations of naughty words whenever that stupid message appeared on *their* monitors – always under the strain of deadline pressure.

But I remained calm. I stayed mellow. I kept my balance.

And the love notes from my system administrator kept arriving, despite my repeated efforts to do the right thing. Late one afternoon, I needed to send an important message to a certain Italian-surnamed CEO before she left on a trip. So I'm under the gun, working feverishly, cranking out the words. I finish the draft, proofread it one more time, then punch "Send."

Nothing happens. The message just sits there. Then this appears:

SYSTEM ADMINISTRATOR WARNING. Your mailbox has exceeded one or more size limits set by your administrator. You may not be able to send or receive mail until you reduce your mailbox size.

It froze me out. I couldn't send the email. The stupid thing froze me out.

If I had been a cartoon, my head would have swollen to three times its size and then exploded. But since I have children and have trained myself not to swear in public, this is what came out of my mouth:

"Dog puppet! Uvula! Santa Cruz! Yankee Doodle!"

At least that's my story and I'm sticking to it.

When I had recovered enough to hold at bay the urge to chuck my monitor through the nearest window, I took a walk through the surrounding cubes, past a meeting where some colleagues were discussing the new seating arrangement for our department.

We're shaking up our little piece of the corporate ant farm, reconfiguring ourselves into tighter quarters to reduce our overhead. You're probably going through it, too: smaller cubicles, shared spaces in sales offices, hosted cubes for visitors.

I don't know how far this trend will go, but I'm concerned that somebody somewhere is presenting a plan to some committee. His idea is to stuff us all into a rack of morgue drawers. That way they can shove the drawers shut at the end of the day and rent the place out as a dance studio at night. Meanwhile, we can grab a few hours of sleep and get back to work when the dancers are through.

It's all for a good cause, I tell myself. We're making ourselves faster, more efficient. We're saving money, putting it into the right opportunities to grow and capture markets. We're funding R&D, putting more feet on the street. I'm all for that. I support it completely.

It's just that I always thought we should treat our workers with respect and provide them with a reasonable

SYSTEM ADMINISTRATOR WARNING. This column has exceeded one or more size limits set by your administrator. You may not be able to finish it until you reduce the number of words. Simply delete 200 words, reboot and sing the Chinese national anthem. And don't bother responding to this message because we won't either.

Note: This penultimate column comes from Tieline East, published way back in the winter of 1991. It's an attempt to describe what drives men and a bit of a plea for peace, as hard as that seems to be in a world driven by economics, revenge and lunatics. Heavy sigh.

It's also about a time long ago when summer meant vacation at a heavenly place in North Carolina with our young children and great friends. Then a basketball game broke out...

Y in the World

Let's just say I wasn't born to play basketball. It's bad enough that I'm short and I'm slow. What's worse is that I have no shot and couldn't out-jump Roseanne Barr in heels.

At 5'9" and 160 pounds, I have the build of a second baseman. Unfortunately, I play ball like a middle linebacker. I relish slamming into people and crashing the boards, though I could use a ladder for the latter.

This tendency toward aggressive play is hardly my fault, thank goodness. The blame lies in a curious genetic aberration peculiar to guys and known in common parlance as "the Y chromosome."

I'll probably get tossed out of the Guy Club of America for admitting this, but our exclusive clump of DNA can cause some positively bizarre behavior.

Take remote controls, for example. Ever watch while a guy controls the remote? We zip through the channels like

Carl Lewis on diet pills, never resting for more than a nanosecond on each one.

That's the famous Y chromosome at work: It can't stand the possibility that somehow, somewhere we might be missing a ball game.

This same chromosome is responsible for our refusal to ask directions when we're lost or the need to turn down the radio when we're searching to find a place – we simply are not wired to do more than one thing at a time. This is in Opposite Town from the X chromosome, which allows female-type beings to concentrate on up to 27 tasks at the same time and accomplish them without strain or fuss.

Our Y chromosome, on the other hand, forces us to drive for miles in hot pursuit of the idiot who cut us off on the freeway, honking the horn, flashing the lights and making the kind of hand signals we would never want our grandmothers to see. Or use, come to think of it.

The Y makes us slam into each other on a basketball court. It makes us want to fight sometimes. But it's not our fault, you realize. It's the stupid chromosome.

Here's an example. One sweltering day last summer, six close friends took their Y's to a nearby, unoccupied beach house that had a basketball backboard, hoop and just enough driveway to serve as a court for some three-on-three. We're pretty typical as guys go: mild-mannered most of the time but capable of being aggressive, intense and very competitive.

Our regular forays into weekend and vacation athletics reflect these latter characteristics. In other words, if we were all better looking and had more hair, we'd make a great beer commercial.

Maybe it was the heat or the stage of the moon, but the competition was more fierce than usual that day. We slammed around the court immersing ourselves in the Three S's of Guydom: Sweating, Swearing and Spitting. Once in a while, someone even made a basket.

At one point my dear friend Tom and I attempted to swap bodies. I was setting a pick, which is an interesting basketball curiosity. It involves standing still and contemplating your life insurance coverage while an enormous person who isn't looking smashes into you.

Tom, who is the size of Montana, had a painful scrape on his arm from previous Guy Sports Combat. When we collided, I accidentally dug my forearm into the wound. He screamed in pain and retaliated in typical Y fashion by shoving me halfway across the court.

Caught up in the welter of battle, I marched back to him spouting combinations of words guaranteed to get you thrown out of Bible school. Tom, who could pound me into bean curd at the slightest provocation, reciprocated until cooler heads arrived to separate us.

Minutes later, Mike and Gary exploded. Some minor transgression set them off and Gary went after Mike like a Rottweiler chasing a man wrapped in bacon. Mike stood his ground and the two of them – fists clenched, neck veins bulging – spit provocative words into each other's face. Cooler heads again prevented fisticuffs among friends.

It was the most violent of the half dozen such skirmishes that marred the game and, to anyone watching, must have made us seem like a half-dozen gorillas fighting a death match. Luckily, the block seemed oddly empty.

After we pulled Mike and Gary apart, two of the milder-mannered among us refused to play anymore. They were justifiably concerned that serious damage to strong friendships was only a hard foul away. So the game disintegrated in anger and we all trudged back to the beach houses we were sharing.

We laugh about it now. Most of us laughed about it a few minutes later, once our bodies stopped making adrenaline and the substance began to break down. Quick to anger, quick to forget – that's the motto of the Y within us.

But take our harmless game a step further. Throw in vastly different cultures, political motives, industry profits and high-tech instruments of death and destruction. Then that same Y chromosome that turns a friendly game into combat becomes a source of terror and tears.

Sixteen wars are raging across the world at the moment, all fueled by the fury of the Y. I have a modest suggestion. Why don't we outlaw the guns of war and encourage soldiers everywhere to exchange their weapons for basketballs. Then we'll find a court someplace and settle these things like men.

Note: I married for a second time on October 4, 2014, to my dearest love, a woman from Caxias do Sul in far southern Brazil. Whenever we've gone somewhere together – both before and after our wedding – people have always asked how we met when we lived so many thousands of miles apart. Here, at last, is the story that proves there is no such thing as coincidences.

How An American Boy Met a Brazilian Girl

How does a man living in Mountain View, California, in the heart of Silicon Valley, meet and fall deeply, madly, spiritually in love with a woman who hails from Caxias do Sul in very southern Brazil, about 7,500 frequent flyer miles away? It's a question Fátima and I are asked wherever we go and here, finally, is the answer.

If the sports book in Las Vegas set the line on the two of us ever meeting, the odds would be at least three billion to one – about the same as finding a specific drop of saltwater in a one-mile stretch off the Northern California Coast or an equal amount off the western edge of the Atlantic below the equator.

What follows is the story of how we overcame these steepest of odds and it begins with an online posting on craigslist in San Francisco, of all places.

It was 2008 and my ex-wife and I had filed the final document ending our marriage more than a year before. I was still getting over the way it ended through admission of my role in the break-up, forgiving my spouse for her

262

transgressions and praying for us both to heal. I readily admit I had more work to do to break through the last of my depression and arrive at acceptance, the last stop in Kubler-Ross's cycle of grief.

One of my all-time favorite artists, Lucinda Williams, happened to be playing with her band at a small venue not too far from my home. So I wrote what I thought was a coherent craigslist message (with actual punctuation, and correct spelling and grammar) and posted it on the men-seeking-women section. The note briefly explained my situation and asked for someone to accompany me to the concert.

Over the next couple of days a handful of offers filtered back, but nothing that made me jump with enthusiasm. I was close to giving up when a very different email appeared in my Inbox.

It looked foreign from the beginning and the sender was a woman named "Fátima." Anything with an accent mark is foreign to those of us who live in the U.S., right? I treated the email as if a strange package had appeared on my porch, picking and prodding at it gently to make sure it didn't explode.

The email address had "tradutora" spliced after Fátima and I had no idea what that meant. I assumed it was her last name or maybe her married name. Or could she be divorced, too? I tried to grasp whatever meaning I could out of clues so faint the bloodhound of Sherlock Holmes would have trouble following them.

I decided to take a chance and double-clicked on the missive, which opened before me like a yellow rose after a summer shower. Inside, I read a lovely note in perfect English. The sender said she appreciated my craigslist posting and would enjoy going with me to see Lucinda. Unfortunately, there was a major encumbrance: She lived in Brazil.

And not just Brazil but southern Brazil. I didn't find out until later exactly how far south Caxias do Sul is. The city of about 400,000 people rests in the state of Rio Grande do Sul (Big River of the South), which is the southernmost of the 26 states comprising Brazil. The state borders Argentina and Uruguay, for goodness' sake.

If you're ever at the home of a friend who happens to have a world globe, you can see just how far south this city is. Also, I don't know why I wasn't aware of this, but South America is much further east than the United States, too. Blame the U.S. public school system.

In her email, Fátima said she likes the way I write and wished she could accompany me to the concert, even though she didn't know anything about Lucinda or her music. She ended by wishing me well and hoping I had a nice time at the event.

There was something about the way she wrote that intrigued me immediately. Fátima was obviously very intelligent (and had a special talent for recognizing good writing, ha ha) and her choice of words showed a soulfulness and depth lacking from the previous candidates for a date.

Her perfect English demonstrated a fluency that could come only from someone who either spent considerable time in the U.S. or had studied the language for years. Finally, she exhibited both a sense of adventure by responding to a craigslist posting from nearly 8,000 miles away and a slight maternal quality that appealed to a lonely, still-healing man in Mountain View.

I let the email sit in my Inbox for a day to ensure it wasn't a mirage. Then I responded, thanking Fátima for her reply, expressing my regret she couldn't make it and telling her how much I enjoyed her email. I closed by suggesting we become cross-continental email pals.

And that's how our story begins, from my side.

Turning to the same event from Fátima's perspective like a mini-Rashomon, she lived with her teenaged son, the youngest of three children, in a condominium in Caxias and worked as a translator ("tradutora") and teacher of English and Portuguese, her native language. Her marriage had ended in a painful way, too, and about the same time that mine did.

A member of her circle of friends told Fátima a woman named Nadia had recently returned to Caxias from two years in the U.S. and was interested in making new friends.

Fátima met Nadia at a group dinner shortly afterwards. To continue exploring this new friendship and to combat her own loneliness, Nadia asked if she could spend the weekend at Fátima's place. Fátima, the kind of person who welcomes strays from all over the taxonomic table – from cats to humans – agreed.

On Saturday night during the weekend, Nadia – an exuberant woman in her 40s – was feeling frisky. She didn't have a male interest in her life and knew that Fátima's 23-year marriage had ended two years before. So Nadia suggested the two women go online and have some fun searching for available men.

While she lived in the U.S., Nadia worked in Mountain View (within a mile or so of where I live, if you like to look for coincidences – which I no longer believe in) for a top Silicon Valley company with a name that rhymes with Zoogle. She suggested they try craigslist in San Francisco, a site Nadia knew from her time in the Bay Area.

For those of you who have never scrolled through craigslist, there are many perfectly fine and useful sections. There are also a few that would make an emergency-room doctor blush. Among the sections for women seeking men, men seeking women, women seeking women and men seeking men who are seeking women, there is one called casual encounters. This latter destination is a place to browse a vast selection of erections so long you could hang your newly washed shirts on them, along with urgent but somewhat less primitive requests to satisfy a woman's carnal urges.

While a couple of playful ladies in Caxias do Sul on a weekend night might admit to scrolling through some of the flag-pole photos, they also reviewed some of the tamer offerings under men seeking women, where I posted my Lucinda invitation.

What a small world this has become through the Internet and social media. From more than a continent away Fátima happened upon the words I had written a few days before and was moved to respond. Although she is fully capable of living happily and productively on her own, she was lonely, too. (Doesn't there seem to be a lot of loneliness in the world?)

For the next year, we sent each other fun, playful emails along with occasional photos. Fátima warned me early on that she didn't look anything like one of the young, trim, nearly naked samba dancers who perform on traveling stages during Carnival in Rio. I assured her that I didn't either.

Then came the afternoon of October 10, 2009. I was clickety-clacking on my keyboard as usual when my landline phone rang. It's a line I rarely answer because it's listed publically and 99.9 percent of the calls I receive are trying to sell me something.

But I looked at the display and saw a long series of numbers with nothing to indicate a marketer had placed the call. So I answered. On the other end a sweetly accented voice on the deep side of feminine said, "Is this David Price the writer?"

I was captivated immediately. We talked briefly, voice to voice, for the first time and it was magical from that moment on. I just love her accent, especially when she says certain words such as "pillow," which usually comes out as "pee-low." It's adorable to me.

Our emails afterward took on a more romantic and sometimes suggestive-yet-still-playful tone and we gravitated to Skype.

Soon we talked at least once or twice a day on that Jetsons-like tool, sharing our daily challenges, hopes and small victories together. I recall a lot of laughter during those video calls. No matter what issues we faced, we talked them through with someone who cared enough to listen attentively and we almost always ended up laughing together.

Finally, I suggested she come up to California. She suggested, better yet, why don't I come visit her?

So I acquired my visa for Brazil, bought my ticket and embarked on a 21-hour-straight airplane trip from San Francisco to Atlanta to Sao Paulo to Porto Alegre, the latter about a two-hour drive from Caxias do Sul. The plan was for Fátima to meet me outside the baggage claim at the Porto Alegre airport.

I arrived on the final leg of this long journey, looking as bedraggled as a long-haired Persian cat subjected to the indignity of a bath. I stumbled into the baggage claim area where about two hundred other people converged, all of them speaking Portuguese much more rapidly than the beginner's CD I had been listening to for the past few months as I drove to work and back.

The baggage carousel turned and turned with fewer pieces of luggage and heavily taped boxes each time around. After 10 more minutes there were only a handful of suitcases left and one slightly battered box. Then the motor shut down bringing everything to a slow, squeaking stop. Great, I thought, my luggage is probably waiting for me in Nova Scotia where another David Price – there are a lot of us – is trying on my underwear.

So I walked over to the luggage help desk, waited my turn and the older of two men behind the counter indicated he was ready to help me.

"Voce fala ingles?" I asked, trying to imitate the accent on the CD.

It worked because he shook his head, letting me know that he did not speak English. But he called over the other, much younger man with a thick, neatly trimmed black beard, who apparently did.

I explained my problem to this young fellow whose English was passable but certainly much better than my attempts at Portuguese. He took my baggage claim number and said he'd get back to me in a few minutes.

While I waited, I decided to wander to the baggage claim exit, poke my head out the double doors and see if I could spot Fátima. Outside, people scurried here and there or talked in small, animated clusters. I scanned the large waiting area, especially the row of wooden benches about 10 meters away. No Fátima.

As I tend to do in these kinds of situations, I began to panic. I now realized I had forgotten to bring Fátima's cell phone number and home address. What an idiot I am! I'm 7,500 miles from home, in a country where I don't speak the language and I'm about to be murdered in a complex scam that I had fallen for hook, line, sinker, pole and pier, too.

I returned to the baggage claim desk and the young fellow wasn't there. I felt as if I were in a Hitchcock movie where the protagonist gets himself deeper and deeper into a maze of his own creation while the killer waits, like a black widow spider, silent now but poised to leap with deadly intent at the slightest tingle of its web.

I lingered five more minutes and when he didn't return I decided to go back and check on Fátima. For the second time, I stuck my head out the baggage claim doors and scanned the waiting area. No Fátima.

Truly panicking by now, I tried to pray and use the tools I had learned recently to calm myself. After taking several long, deep breaths of sparkling, healing air and exhaling as slowly as I took them in, the panic began to subside. As it did, the young fellow appeared from behind another doorway and waved for me to come over.

"I think maybe we have found them," he said and I hoped he meant my one suitcase.

He beckoned for me to follow him to yet another doorway in the large baggage room and wait outside. He entered and I stood there for another few minutes, practicing my breathing exercise.

He finally emerged, carrying my suitcase.

"Is this one your luggage?" he asked.

It was indeed.

"Muito obrigado," I replied, thanking him very much.

"De nada," he replied, with a brilliant white smile that contrasted starkly with his black-onyx beard. "Have a successful visit."

I loaded my suitcase onto the four-wheeled, triangular-shaped luggage cart you could use for free, unlike the $5 charge in most U.S. airports. I'd already placed my backpack stuffed with my camera bag inside and laptop computer case on this small metal camel and used the cart to transport my small stack of gear toward the baggage claim doorway.

As I exited, pushing my belongings in front of me like a man on a pilgrimage to the Holy Land, I took another soothing breath and glanced at the wooden benches to my right. All around them people moved this way and that, a welter of greetings, smiles and even some tears.

I glanced to my right and the only thing I saw in that entire room was a pair of exquisite eyes, with a lovely touch of makeup accentuating the soft brown irises.

They were the most beautiful eyes I had ever seen: at least a step larger than average, colorful and expressive. These were the eyes of an angel, a fairy and a goddess – all wonderfully blended into human form. What made them even more striking was that they were looking right back at me.

Her eyes moved suddenly as Fátima rose from the bench and walked over to greet me. I have no idea what we said to each other, but I will always remember the hug and the warmth of her body. Despite my additional three inches of height, we seemed to fit together as if we were two halves of the same ripe Georgia peach. It was as if I were the mythological lover lost at sea that Neptune decided to cough up and return unhurt to the shore where Fátima waited faithfully.

That's how we met in person. During the next four-plus years, I visited her nine times for about 12 days each. We had such great fun meeting her children and adoring friends, traveling to family events and touring southern Brazil including the soul-restoring beach at Pereque, the German architecture and possibility of snow that Gramado offers, our delightful romantic hideaway above the waters of Porto Belo, and the glorious sand, clouds and waves surrounding the island city of Florianopolis.

We turned out to be natural traveling companions in her older model, bluish-grey Picasso. Fátima is a superb storyteller with a wealth of insight into people and how they react to one another and I relish listening to good stories. On an early trip I fished out a battered Peter, Paul and Mary CD, popped it into the player and we bonded further by singing along to everything from "Don't Think Twice It's Alright" to "Leaving on a Jet Plane."

We made love for the first time in a small hotel room in Porto Alegre – I recall a lot of white – and it was so sweet, passionate and reciprocal that my eyes nearly dropped tears of joy.

Fátima came to the States to see me about twice a year, staying anywhere from two weeks to more than a month. Our love grew deeper and stronger during these years. And although I never thought I would wed a second time, I asked her to marry me, at least three times that I remember. She answered each query with the word "yes," except for the one time she responded, "Of course," which made me laugh out loud and realize there was never any question about it.

Epilogue

I was about to visit Fátima in southern Brazil for the 10th time in April 2014, but had to postpone the trip because of some unusual lung problems I was having, beginning in early 2014. Then came May 28, 2014, which I discuss in the Prologue to this book. It's the day my pulmonologist told me I had end-stage, metastasized cholangiocarcinoma (bile duct cancer) and only had a month or two to live.

I shared this news with Fátima and my children and it was devastating to us all. I have a wonderful relationship with my kids, who are well established in their college careers, and we cried long and hard together.

I was introduced to an oncologist for the first time in my life and she immediately put me on the schedule to start chemotherapy to treat this rare cancer (only 2,000 to 3,000 cases are diagnosed in the U.S. each year), using gemcitabine and cisplatin as the main agents. The doctor later told me that fewer than 30 percent of patients with this particular cancer respond favorably to the treatment.

Fátima planned to come see me as soon as she could arrange it, including temporarily leaving her job with the Juvenile Court System of Caxias where she worked in Restorative Justice, which focuses on restoring relationships between offenders and victims for the benefit of the entire community instead of simply relying on sentencing and punishment. It's a cause she remains passionate about.

On June 13, I arrived at the Infusion Center in Palo Alto, California, and one of the angelic, highly skilled healthcare professionals who work there inserted an IV into my right arm about 8:45 in the morning to begin the nine-hour session of running various and sometimes nasty chemicals through my veins.

Through whatever cosmic connection we share, it was the same day Fátima arrived in the States. My daughter Ellery, home from college, picked her up at the San Francisco airport. These essential women in my life arrived at the Infusion Center together around 12:30 p.m. I took turns hugging them, doing the best a fellow can who has an IV piercing his right arm.

The year 2014 has ended and I was supposed to be dead by the end of last July. My guess is that my Higher Power knows I have more work to do – including finishing this book, fostering many important relationships and giving back as much as I possibly can – that he's extended my life on earth considerably.

Most days I have a wonderful attitude. I've accepted my disease but do my best not to let it dictate how I feel and how I treat people. I try to live each day to the fullest, spending time writing, playing guitar (something I always wanted to do but didn't have the time), visiting with friends, going to AA meetings and trying to support the important people in my life. A lot of my time is devoted to Fátima, who is still here beside me.

I almost died twice during the early days of chemotherapy before we backed off on the treatment frequency. However, I've felt so good for much of the past three months that I asked Fátima one more time to marry me back in September. Not only did she agree, but we actually carried out our spontaneous wedding plans in only three weeks' time with the help of some wonderful friends and a lot of luck, if you still want to call it that.

We initially decided to wed in a simple ceremony at the county clerk's office in nearby Redwood City; however, the idea never seemed to fit the occasion. So we progressed at warp speed to a full church wedding with bride's maids and groom's assistants, essential guests, email invitations and RSVPs, specially chosen and performed live music, flowers, plenty of food and cake, and so much happy chatter – all in a hectic, near miraculous three weeks.

With 70 dear friends and family members looking on and pledging their support, Fátima and I married on October 4, 2014.

One of my favorite activities is to look back at all the selected photos (winnowed down to about 200 from the original 796). I especially like one of my daughter, Ellery, and son, Owen, prancing out of the church together (both were in the wedding party) with huge smiles on their faces. And, of course, the beautiful shots of my loving bride as we took our vows and lit the unity candle while the minister and a friend traded piano and guitar licks to the Karla Bonoff version of the classic song "The Water is Wide."

It's been important for me to learn fairly early how tough life can be and that it can bring you down to your knees in sadness and despair sometimes. I've had lifelong issues with chronic illness, depression and addiction, and finally got clean and sober beginning in August 2005.

I have also experienced many occasions overflowing with laughter, love and so much beauty that they can bring you to tears from the other side of the Libran scales.

What I know now is that it's essential for me to accept the things in life I can't control, always bearing in mind that I can control how I react to them. Of course, I'm going to break down when I hear the news that I don't have long to live. It's only natural. I can only imagine how much worse it must be for people who are younger than I am at 62 years of age.

I try not to wallow in it for long because I know it's a waste of precious time. Grief is important but I remember that the final phase of grieving is acceptance.

Meanwhile, when I'm feeling low, I make a gratitude list. Even if it only has such items as: roof over head, running water, bed to sleep in, the contented purr of our cats, nice ergonomic chair to sit in while I type, I realize so many people in the world don't have even these small comforts.

I know I only have a limited amount of time left on this planet. But as long as the combination of western medicine and multi-denominational prayer from my family and friends all over the world continues to work, I have hope. And that's the most important four-letter word in the language.

Peace and love,
David L. Price
January 2015

At Last, They Marry

If I have to choose one photo from October 4, 2014, to demonstrate the enduring love I share with Fátima and how our story continues, it's this one. It features my lovely bride (left) and the fellow with the bald spot.

Although this is a great photo, too, starring my children, Ellery and Owen...

About the Author

Photograph by Fátima De Bastiani

David L. Price is a professional writer living in Mountain View, California. He has worked in Employee Communications for major international corporations, including Hewlett-Packard, Gilead Sciences and Hitachi. During this time, David has written hundreds of feature articles and blog postings for employee websites. He has won many top awards for his writing, including the Gold Quill Award from IABC, the Award of Distinction from the Communicator and 17 Command Performance in Communication awards from Hewlett-Packard.

David also has published short humor articles professionally, including pieces for Hemispheres, the in-flight magazine from United Airlines, and Denver magazine. He finished writing and editing his first novel, *Slugger*, in fall 2013, and published it in 2014.

Apparently So, his second book, is a compilation of many of the short articles he has written, including some from his work at Hewlett-Packard. He wrote the majority of the articles in his "spare time."

You can visit David's website and subscribe to his new writing at www.davidpriceapparentlyso.com

About the Others Who Helped

The Illustrators: *Alex Carr is a watercolor artist in rural Loudoun County, Virginia, who holds a Bachelor of Arts degree in Studio Art from Wellesley College. She owns and operates the Alex Carr Art Studio, a spacious working studio with a large, state-of-the-art classroom.*

Alex has been represented by galleries in Colorado, New Mexico, Virginia and New York City. A critical review of her paintings appears in the spring 2013 issue of ArtisSpectrum, a New York publication that profiles contemporary art and artists.

Alex's commercial art and illustration experience spans numerous venues, some of which include greeting cards, wine labels, t-shirt designs and most recently a poster series for craft beer.

Mira Dabrowski is a software training and research professional who also dabbles in doodling and music (singing her favorite folk, country and rock n' roll tunes with musician friends) while, as a single mom, sharing the job of raising twins who are now in their third year of college.

Despite her beloved high school art teacher's best efforts, Mira says she "managed to miss out on some key concepts." Yet she has forged ahead, delighting family and friends over the years with hand-drawn cards for the holidays and other art projects.

The Graphic Designer: *Sarah Mattern is a delight to work with and has helped me tremendously by designing my website; the cover of Slugger, my first book; and the cover and layout for Apparently So.*

Sarah is a graphic designer and front-end web developer. She says that she "designs information and builds interfaces to help people create, connect and discover." You can learn more at matternco.com.

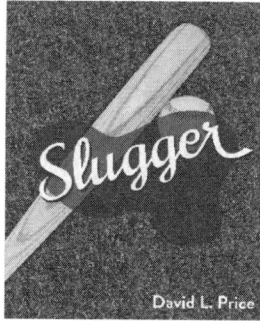

David L. Price's first book is **Slugger,** a novel about a young woman trapped in an increasingly abusive relationship and how she discovers a way out. The action is set against a backdrop of the Colorado plains outside Denver, professional baseball, drug and alcohol addiction, and the miracle of recovery.

Both **Slugger** and **Apparently So** are available online at www.davidpriceapparentlyso.com

Made in the USA
San Bernardino, CA
17 March 2015